Praise for Unspoken Conversations

There are many negative events which can occur in life that cause a need for restoration. As you journey through these pages, you will be inspired by the author's story, and be compelled to delve deep into your soul so that you, like her, can understand who you really are and be transformed into the beautiful masterpiece you were created to be.

~ Dr. Kisia L. Coleman, M.O.D.E.L. (Mentoring Our Daughters, Equipping Ladies) Ministries, Founder, Kingdom Church Int'l., Co-Founder, Chicago, IL

In reading this book, I witnessed artistry in motion as Rakisha tells her highly gut-wrenching story which uncurls gently, handling the emotionally-charged events which shaped her life and her soul. An enlightening and encouraging must-read that demonstrates the power of God's love over acts of abuse in determining the outcome of what seemingly appeared to be defining life-destructive events. How she identified life's distractions, maintained her focus, kept her sanity, and evolved as a stronger and wiser person is a model worthy of following.

~ Rev. Dr. Esther M. Rose, AME Zion Church, Tomball, TX

Unspoken Conversations is a book I would recommend to anyone who wants a steadfast approach to wholeness and healing through God's Word. Rakisha spoke from a place of pain that led her to live a life of deliverance in God. The stability of God's Word illuminates in each chapter, as it leads readers to a place in God where love resides.

~ Abbey Shaw, MSCIS, CISSP, Information Technology/Cybersecurity Professional, Detroit, MI

Riveting, inspirational, and insightful, this expression amplifies the tumultuous journey experienced by a young woman's quest to unveil the secrecy of relational abuse, its effects, and the compelling intervention of Jesus Christ that redirected her to healing, self-worth, and wholeness.

~ Elizabeth Anderson, MAPC, Professional Counseling Services, Houston, TX

I see the result of a life that chose to trust God. In *Unspoken Conversations*, the butterfly effect came about by faith, resilience, and endurance, resulting in true transformation and healing. What an inspiration to all who will read it to trust God and His Word. Thank you for sharing your journey with us. You are an inspiration of courage, faith, and strength. I'm so honored to call you my friend!

~ Patty Ridings, TV Host of the Patty Ridings Show and CFO at Family Harvest Church, Tinley Park, IL

If you've ever wondered why your internal desires, goals, and dreams were not realities in your life, this book is for you. *Unspoken Conversations* is a narrative road map to discovering your true self. Rakisha masterfully and candidly takes readers on a journey of liberty and harmony. The spirit between the lines of this book facilitates healing and awakening to the possibilities of greatness that lies in each of us.

> ~ **Lildella Douglas, M.Ed., LPC, NCC, Spirit of Excellence Consulting, Founder, Orland Park, IL**

Unspoken Conversations will keep you on the edge of your seat, as you journey through the life of Dr. Rakisha Vinegar from an early age to now. She encountered pain, setbacks, and challenges that were meant to take her down a path of destruction, only to emerge as a beautiful, strong, and confident woman on the other side. For people that have been through and/or are going through sexual, emotional, and relational abuse, this book is a must-read. Dr. Rakisha gives you tangible steps and tools to heal spiritually, emotionally, and how to leave behind abusive relationships and move forward to love, hope, and a bright future.

> ~ **Ericka G. Moore, Author of Memoirs of Singlehood, Tinley Park, IL**

Unspoken Conversations is a book that takes you on Dr. Vinegar's lifelong journey of searching for answers, finding hope and healing, and becoming a mature woman of God. This book is an excellent read, with raw emotion and examples of her unwavering faith. Expect to learn how she relentlessly pursued a deeper walk with God in the midst of tremendous change, loss, and difficult times.

Over the years, I have watched Dr. Vinegar make tough decisions for herself and her daughter. In this book, she takes it a step further. She allowed herself to become vulnerable and share her stories of relational abuse so that we can learn and grow. She shares intimate details of her life so that we too can ask ourselves thought-provoking questions. Get your copy of this book. You will be inspired and challenged to answer a question we can all relate to: "What should I do now?" Her life shows us that we don't have to face this question with fear and trepidation. Instead, she shows us how we can also be courageous, tenacious, and put our trust in God. Dig in. Let this book help you take off rose-colored glasses in areas of your life and embark on a path to wholeness.

~ **Tasha Weatherspoon, PT, MPT, GCS, Allied Health Services, Ford Heights, IL**

This powerful book is filled with courage, honesty, and, above all, confidence. Many themes run throughout. One is the witness of the calm before the storm. Dr. Rakisha takes us on a journey once known as her marriage that at times mirror the scenes of a blockbuster movie. However, unlike in most movies the heroine has the grace of God on her side. Her steps to recovery ring clear and true because she knows the territory intimately in all its pain and promise and has given us the gift of sharing it. This affirming message of hope and healing is a must read.

~ **Coach Syl, Best Selling Author, Accountability Coach & Thought Leader**

Dr. Rakisha's intellectual property, *Unspoken Conversations*, is the antithesis of "Survivor's Remorse." This book will gently awaken a voice forced into silence. The intimate accounts and transparency from a voice formerly unheard will not only deepen your thoughts about abuse but will also stir the courage within to procure and loudly declare victory.

~ **Elder Tif Simmons, Prophetic Winds Production, Co-Owner, Chicago, IL**

Unspoken CONVERSATIONS

AN INNER DIALOGUE TO SELF-DISCOVERY AND FREEDOM FROM RELATIONAL ABUSE

DR. RAKISHA A. VINEGAR

Published by KishKnows Publishing
Visit the author's website at
http://www.drrakisha.com/

Printed in the United States of America
ISBN: 978-0-692-12225-9
LCCN: 2018905904

All rights reserved. No part of this book may be reproduced in any form by any electronic or mechanical means, including photocopying, recording, or information storage and retrieval without permission in writing from the author.

Unless otherwise indicated, all Scripture quotations are taken from the Holy Bible, **New King James Version**® **(NKJV)**. Copyright © 1982. Used by permission of Thomas Nelson. All rights reserved.

Scripture quotations marked **NIV** are taken from the Holy Bible, **New International Version.** Copyright © 1973, 1978, and 1984 by International Bible Society. Used by permission of Zondervan Publishing House. All rights reserved.

Scripture quotations marked **MSG** are taken from **The Message.** Copyright © 1993, 1994, 1995, 1996, 2000, 2001, 2002, 2003 by Eugene H. Peterson. Used by permission of NavPress Publishing Group.

Scripture quotations designated **AMP** are taken from **Amplified Bible. Copyright** © 1973, 1978, and 1984 by International Bible Society. Used by permission of Zondervan Publishing House. All rights reserved.

Scriptures taken from **The Voice**™. Copyright © 2008 by Ecclesia Bible Society.

Used by permission. All rights reserved.

Scriptures taken from **GOD'S WORD**®, Copyright © 1995 God's Word to the Nations.

Used by permission of Baker Publishing Group. All rights reserved.

Scripture taken from the **Modern English Version**. Copyright © 2014 by Military Bible Association. Used by permission. All rights reserved.

ADVISORY

Readers are advised to consult with their physician or another professional practitioner if they are, or believe they may be, involved in an abusive situation. This book is not intended to take the place of professional advice, medical or otherwise. Neither the author nor the publisher assumes any liability for possible adverse consequences as a result of the information contained herein.

Dedication

To all the daughters…and the FATHER who loves them…
You are a Daddy's Girl!

For the Father Himself [tenderly] loves you…
          John 16:27 (AMP)

Contents

Preface: Never in a Million Years xiii
Introduction: The Butterfly Effect of an Unspoken
    Conversation xv

Part I: The Beginning Conversation 1
Chapter 1:   I – Identity 3
Chapter 2:   A – Acceptance 11
Chapter 3:   M – Meaning 17

Part II: The Learning Conversation 23
Chapter 4:   C - Confidence 25
Chapter 5:   O – Optimism 35
Chapter 6:   U – Understanding 41

Part III: The Surviving Conversation 51
Chapter 7:   R – Resilience 53
Chapter 8:   A – Ashes 61
Chapter 9:   G – Gratitude 73
Chapter 10: E – Empowered 83

Part IV: The Thriving Conversation 101
Chapter 11: O – Overcoming 103
Chapter 12: U – Unwavering 113
Chapter 13: S – Stable 121
From This Day Forward 131

Appendices **139**
Appendix A: My Identity – A Prayer of Redemption 141
Appendix B: My Healing – A Prayer of Restoration 143
Appendix C: My Victory 145
Appendix D: My New Wings! 147

Notes 149
Acknowledgements 155
Resources for Help 157
About the Author 161

Preface

Never in a Million Years

There comes a time in your life when you become fully persuaded that you have made the right decision to live and walk by faith. You become fully persuaded that you are loved. While my journey has always been one of hope, and making lemonade out of lemons, I do experience times of uncertainty. I can honestly say that I had a lot of hesitation when it came to the desire to write this book, mainly because I really did not want to face the buried pain of my past. I also did not know how to face this pain because I had developed my own coping mechanisms. I had come to the point where I had buried the pain, thinking I was healed, or used my favorite quote, "I'm good!" But this was only partially true. I was good… but I was not fully healed. You see, God's desire is for us to be whole, and I was just "surviving" my way through life. After I started this journey of penning my story, I got excited about it. I saw God begin to use my pen to tell my story for His Glory. It is my prayer that my story blesses you and helps you on an even greater journey of discovery and restoration (recovery) as you heal from your past and embrace your future. I am excited about your journey and I am ready to go with you!

In His Grip…Rakisha

Introduction

The Butterfly Effect of an Unspoken Conversation

"For everything that happens in life –
There is a season, a right time for
everything under heaven:
…A time to be quiet, a time to speak up."

Ecclesiastes 3:1, 7 (VOICE)

Throughout our lives, we experience various types of "alternations" or "rotations." These changes usually occur during different timeframes or, as I like to call them, *life seasons*. When we go through seasonal changes, (for example, moving from fall to winter), we don't continue wearing summer clothes (unless it's a favorite shirt). When seasons change, we also change; for this reason, we need to recognize when there has been a seasonal change. For me, I was significantly affected because I was not *aware* of my seasons, let alone when they were changing.

God's Plans and Purposes

In my early childhood, I began forming walls to protect myself from external dangers. These walls manifested into internal conversations. Although they were designed to protect me, the communication was one-directional and catered to preserving my pain in the absence of delivering the truth. The monologues that began at a young age followed me into my young adult years. For years, I waited for my voice to give me the assurance that could only come from God. Each life season of change birthed an inner conversation that allowed me to move forward. However, I still had many unanswered questions.

Have you ever found yourself in the middle of a situation and wondered how in the world you got there? Or where the help was when you needed it? I have had many times where help seemed too far away to reach or lay hold of. Throughout my twenties, I believed the direction I was going in was secure, and I thought I had a solid understanding of who I was. However, I began to realize that this path had slowly placed me on an intricate path of self-discovery and knowing God. I want to show you how *self-awareness* became a focal point for how I developed a healthy sense of being and a personal relationship with God.

My Butterfly Effect

As I reflect on my journey to restoration, I liken it to the transformation of a butterfly. The butterfly goes through four distinctive changes that are required for it to reach its final stage of maturity: egg, caterpillar, cocoon, and adult. My transformation involved many internal conversations that I used to process events that occurred in my life. While there were many internal conversations, I specifically remember *four pivotal unspoken conversations* that were instrumental in my quest of seeking purpose and fulfillment in God.

This book is a memoir of my journey to restoration. It is my intent as you read this book that you would take note of the areas of your own life where transformation and refinement are needed. I desire that as you look through these pages and find ways to apply these lessons to your own life, you see the hand of God and how He carried me through difficulties, heartbreaks, and victories.

Distinctive Seasonal Conversations

I have divided *Unspoken Conversations* into four parts that will show you how God literally transformed me in such a way that I am humbled by it every day. You will see how I went from an insecure little girl to a courageous woman of God.

The Four Parts

- **"The Beginning Conversation"** (the "egg stage"): three chapters that lay the foundation of how my *identity, acceptance,* and *meaning of existence* was formed.
- **"The Learning Conversation"** (the "caterpillar stage"): these chapters begin to build upon my foundation.

Here I talk about how my *confidence, optimism,* and *understanding of my belief system* were shaped based on my beginning conversation.

- **"The Surviving Conversation"** (the "cocoon stage"): I talk about *being resilient, examining my ashes, developing gratitude,* and *becoming empowered.*

- **"The Thriving Conversation"** (the "adult stage"): I talk about how I *overcame challenges, developed unwavering faith,* and *became stable.*

Getting Started

As you read my story, I want you to imagine yourself being transformed into the person you were created to be. This process may require digging up some things that have been buried very deeply. Often, we push back from going too deeply into our past, but this process of digging brings peace and wholeness that will help you to become victorious.

At the end of each chapter, there is a ***Dialogue for Digging In*** section with questions that will help you go deeper. Do me a favor, and do not pick your "butterfly wing" colors just yet. Let yourself experience the restoration process — however long it takes. This process is not a "fast food drive-thru" or "microwave dinner" journey, so be sure not to move too quickly.

The first thing you need to do is decide to *stay the course,* no matter how difficult it gets. Your story may be similar to what you will read in these chapters, or it may be very different. Whatever the case, we all have places in our lives where healing is needed.

If you have experienced any type of trauma or abuse, you will be able to relate to my story. If you do not have trauma or abuse in your past, praise God! But that doesn't mean that you don't need healing in other areas of your life.

Here you will find a place to heal, regardless of your personal situation. Whatever your situation, you are currently in need of restoration, however, you may not be quite sure how to put your finger on the restoration that you need. Let me help you. I spent most of my twenties and early thirties trying to figure out why I was having so many challenges in my relationships - specifically my marriage. I have since discovered that *having a healthy inner dialogue* and *getting the unspoken conversations out in the open* has been instrumental in my healing and restoration process.

We are about to explore how your *identity* is the foundation of your life. We will discover together how to go from *mistaken identity* to *complete restoration* by establishing a healthy inner dialogue. We will go from *broken and lost* to *thriving*. Get ready! You are going to be amazed at how beautiful your new wings will look once you experience being fully restored to the One who first loved you!

I would suggest having a journal for your thoughts. Just know that this is a safe place for you to be transparent and vulnerable, where you can make the decision to embrace healing and let go of the hurt. If you have a close friend, you can invite them to join you.

> **WARNING!**
>
> *This may be a place where you have never gone. I want you to know that the One who loves you more than anything can be trusted with your heart, and it is OK to surrender to Him. He will never break or abuse you — He is already so in love with you!*

PART I
The Beginning Conversation

"You have been created in order that you might make a difference. You have within you the power to change the world."

~ **Andy Andrews**

These first three chapters encompass the initial stage of my transformation. As it relates to the butterfly, this is the *egg stage*. The cool thing about butterfly eggs is that the female butterfly lays many eggs to ensure they will survive. The eggs are laid in a secure place near the leaves of where they will hatch. Your *environment* is critical at this stage.

Come along with me as I take you through my egg stage, where my **beginning conversation** occurred. We will go through *identity, acceptance,* and *meaning*. Remember! No microwaving on this journey! Take your time to dig in and let go.

Chapter One

I - Identity

> "For everything that happens in life –
> There is a season, a right time for
> everything under heaven:
> A time to be born…"
>
> Ecclesiastes 3:1-2 (VOICE)

We have been created for a specific purpose. Most of us spend our lives trying to figure out what this purpose is. We go to school, get training, and do any number of things to discover our purpose. To be able to know what our purpose is, we must first know *who we are*. We must know our *true identity*. Where do we begin with knowing our true identity? Your identity is the very foundation that you begin to build your life on.

In the beginning stage of transformation, you set the very core of who you are. When we are born, we take on our own identity. This identity is shaped by any number of things. Experiences, trauma, abuse, family background, environment, geographical location, and religion can all play a part in shaping our identity. *Identity* and *personality* are two different things, however, many times, people mistake their *personality* for their *identity*. Our personality is "the combination of characteristics or qualities that form our distinctive character," while our identity is defined as "the fact of being whom or what a person or thing is." In essence, your identity is *who you are* while your personality is the *character* of who you are.

My Identity in the Beginning

When I think about my identity, I have vivid memories of growing up with both of my parents at home. My parents were trendsetters, and ahead of themselves concerning the visions and dreams they had for our family. They wanted to do things differently from how they were brought up. I can recall my mom saying they wanted to change the "bloodline" for their family. My dad was raised Catholic, and my mom was raised Baptist. While my dad went to church growing up and was an altar boy, he questioned his faith once he became a young adult. My mom went to church with her aunts; however, she also questioned her beliefs as a young adult. They met in 1973, married in 1974, and I was born in 1975 in Detroit, Michigan. Together they had three children. My brother was born in 1977, and my sister was born in 1981. I also have an older sister born to my dad before my parents were married.

After I was born, they were faced with a challenge that would shape the foundation on which they would raise their children. I was hospitalized at the age of two because of a calcium deficiency.

Because my parents practiced a vegetarian diet, they did not give me regular cow's milk when I turned two. They made my milk from scratch using nuts, and the problem was that the milk was missing a key component of calcium, and this is how the deficiency occurred. The doctors told my parents that I was not going to grow. They wanted to do surgery on my legs to correct the bone structure, but my parents would not allow it. I wore special shoes to bed that had a brace to correct my feet, and one night, I could not get up to go to the bathroom because of the braces. I remember that was the last night wearing those shoes. I am happy my parents did not go through with the surgery, as none of the doctor's findings came to pass; however, because they did not want me to have the surgery, they were threatened with a lawsuit to take me away from them. In order to get legal help for their case, my father enlisted help from a religious organization known as The Moorish Science Temple of America. The premise behind this organization is that "African Americans are descendants of Moorish Empire, which makes you Moorish by nationality and Islamic by faith." This group helped people who would adopt their beliefs and take on a particular last name, so to receive help from them, he changed our last name to be recognized with this group, and thus began this new bloodline. My parents followed the legal advice given to them and won their case. Although the new name was taken at this time, it was several years before it was changed legally.

What's in a name?

This was a very bold decision for my dad to make, but at the time he thought it was his best option. This name change was not a minor thing. It reminds me of the scene in the movie *Coming to America*, when the man in the barber shop says, "His mama named him Clay, Imma call him Clay!"

It took a very long time before my granddad would call my dad by his new name, and not only did he change his last name, he and my mom also changed their first names. They were taking on a new identity that was different from their childhood, and it took a while before I realized the significance of this. Historically speaking, the last name of a man is the legacy or heritage of the family. In this case, my dad was inadvertently telling my granddad that he did not want to be part of his legacy, and he was also beginning to embrace a new identity.

My Parents…the Trendsetters

This new identity was grounded in both culture and religion. Because my parents were very aware of their African heritage, they desired to instill this awareness in their children. They enrolled me and my brother in a private school whose focus was on "thinking globally, where the African American child could view themselves as the norm" (Wells, 2016).

I completed both kindergarten and first grade there, and my brother completed preschool. At this time, I do not recall following a particular religion. I only remember going to school, and on the weekends, we would do fun things like going to museums. We also had fun around the house. I remember waking up Saturday mornings with Stevie Wonder playing while my mom and dad would clean the house.

When I was in the first grade, my parents opened the first health food store in our neighborhood. It was the coolest thing! My father, with the help of others, built the store from the ground up. If I had to make a comparison, our health food store was the "Whole Foods" of the 1980s. In their case, location was important, and the location was not in an area where people thought about eating healthy. Because it was ahead of its time, business did not pick up, and by the end of my first-grade school year, my parents had to close the store.

The Switch – Phase 1

Up until this point, I was an average seven-year-old, and life was pretty normal as far as I could tell. Something happened about the time I was to enter second grade — my parents changed our school. My brother and I were placed in another private school.

It was not like our first school — this school was specifically for Muslim children. I mentioned earlier about my dad changing our last name and adopting a new identity, but there had been no practicing of Islam up to this point. We were also not identifying with the Moorish culture. There are two major sects or branches of Islam: Sunni and Shiite. We followed the Sunni interpretation, which is based on the belief that the Prophet Muhammad died without appointing a successor to lead the Muslim community.

I remember going from wearing regular school clothes to wearing a uniform consisting of a long brown skirt with a yellow shirt, and having to cover my hair. This was a huge change for our family. My identity was now being shaped by our religion. I was somewhat unclear about who I was, because we went from not talking about or practicing any specific religion to changing everything that I had thought was normal, including the way I dressed. Even at this age, my parents began laying the foundation of my identity. I did not realize it then, but at the age of eight, I was beginning to have an identity crisis. This was when my unspoken conversations began to form.

Identity Crisis – What is it?

Now that you know that identity is "who a person is", have you thought about your identity as the foundation of who you are? Have you ever taken the time to assess the importance of being able to know who you are? We are going to look at some areas where our identity can be challenged. We will also look at how to recover our identity.

What does it mean to have an "identity crisis" or a "mistaken identity?" The first area we can experience mistaken identity is when we try to be someone we are not. It occurs because we do not understand who we are, and we begin to compare ourselves to others in a negative way.

When I talk about life changes, I am speaking of what happened to me when I went from practicing no specific religion to embracing a new religion and customs that were different. For me, I never wanted to be the child that could not talk about what they believed or express themselves to others.

It is important to understand *who you are* and *what you have been created to do*. The foundation for *who you are* is built based on your *identity*. After this, your personality has a part to play as well. Have you taken the time to think about what your foundation is built on? Do you know how to test your foundation for any sinkholes? To test your foundation, take a look at how you respond to life challenges. What foundation did your parents lay for you as a child? Have you been able to build on your childhood foundation?

Stolen Identity – Who takes it?

The second area where our identity is challenged is by way of "stealing" it. Identity theft is a crime that is committed more often than we know.

According to Javelin Strategy and Research, every two seconds, someone's identity is stolen. The thief I am referring to here is the devil. You may be wondering, "How can the devil steal my identity?" Easy! He does not want you to discover who you are and your life's purpose! His primary goal is to steal, kill, and destroy, and he does it very subtly. We have to be mindful of his wicked ways and outsmart him. So how do we protect ourselves from identity theft? Here are some practical ways to protect yourself:

- **Make sure** you are not undergoing an identity crisis.
- **Surround yourself** with positive people.
- **Watch** how you talk to yourself.
- **Meditate** daily on God's word.

Reclaimed Identity – How do we get it back?

When you have tested your foundation and unmasked the thief, it is time to reclaim your identity. How do you get your identity back? There are several steps we can take when we are seeking to reclaim our identity.

- **Understand your authority and power**: You literally have the power of the King of the Universe behind you!

- **Paint a new self-portrait**: Get comfortable looking at yourself in the mirror!

- **Speak positive thoughts** about yourself! This is not denying your situation. It is *changing the way you view your situation.* There is power in your words!

> *Our identity is the foundation of who we are. It is important to know that you matter and you were created for a purpose. Take some time to take inventory of your purpose and who you are. What keeps you up at night and what problems do you enjoy solving?*

Dialogue for Digging In!

1. Have you ever experienced an identity crisis?

2. Are you able to pinpoint any childhood events (both positive and negative) that have shaped your identity? If so, what are those events?

3. If you were raised in a Christian home, what did that look like? Did you go to church as a family? If you were not raised in a Christian home, what did that look like?

4. What are some of the most challenging moments you have encountered, and have you ever taken the time to acknowledge the pain caused by these challenges?

5. Who (or what) is your primary source of comfort?

6. What have you done in the last 30 days to create purpose and vision in your life, and in the lives of others?

Chapter Two

A – Acceptance

> "For everything that happens in life –
> There is a season, a right time for
> everything under heaven:
> …A time to build up"
>
> **Ecclesiastes 3:1, 3 (VOICE)**

Now that we have an understanding of the importance of our identity and how it shapes our foundation, we will begin to add to our foundation by looking at *acceptance*. We all want to be accepted. The dictionary defines acceptance as "the action or process of being received as adequate or suitable, typically to be admitted into a group." It is very important for children to know they are accepted. Acceptance is another layer in your foundation that cannot be ignored. With the switch in our religion and a new school, I began to question whether or not I was accepted by society and even within our religious community.

The Switch – Phase 2

Being the new kid in school, I had to adjust to new people, new structure, new everything. Boys sat on one side of the classroom and girls sat on the other side. The curriculum was the traditional elementary curriculum, and we also learned the different standards and customs of Islam.

One of these standards was the Five Pillars of Islam. These pillars are the principles by which a Muslim lives their life. They are *faith*, *prayer*, *charity*, *fasting*, and *pilgrimage to Mecca*.

As an eight-year-old girl, I remember wanting to know more about Islam. I do not recall having the conversation with my parents at this age about our religion; I only remember going to this new school. At school, I learned about our religion and if I had any questions, I would have to had asked my dad and I didn't. During this time, I remember my parents telling us to call them "Abu" and "Umi", which mean "Dad" and "Mom" in Arabic. That was different for us, but we did it (it wasn't like we were going to say no). This was one of the new things that came with being a Muslim; we began using Arabic words, phrases, and prayers.

The Beginning Conversation

After learning the Five Pillars of Islam, I began to wonder how I was going to live out these principles. Let me explain. Women (or in my case, a young girl), were not allowed to do the same things as the men and boys. Women were not allowed to worship in the same space as the men, nor were we allowed to learn Arabic anywhere but at home or school. We had to know how to read the Quran in Arabic, and we also had to memorize the last ten books in the Quran.

I did not have a conversation with my parents about our religion at this age (8), but I did have the conversation with myself. My first pivotal unspoken conversation occurred when

I was in the second grade. **My first pivotal conversation**: "Why are we doing this? What do these Five Pillars mean and how can we follow them if we are not allowed to go to the mosque? Why can't women go to the mosque and learn like the men?" This was my first conversation, and it turned into continuous conversations as I tried to find the answers to my questions. These questions did not get answered, and I had to accept this even though I knew there was so much more I wanted to know.

This became a form of communication with myself — it was how I learned to process the things going on in my world. These communications became my unspoken voice. I was always told that children were to be seen and not heard, and unfortunately, I believed this and embraced this way of thinking. This had some side effects. My sense of my own identity and self-acceptance was formed based on our religion, and my unspoken conversations were a direct result of being afraid to vocalize my feelings, emotions, and thoughts.

A Surprising Turn

I am not sure what happened, but during the middle of my third-grade school year, my mother left my dad, and we moved in with my grandparents in Chicago. At the time, I did not know what separation or divorce was, but my parents were now separated. I was not even aware of anything going on, because they had been able to shield us from the problems that they were having.

I remember the latter part of third grade very well. It was winter and very cold and snowy! Once again, I was the new kid in school. One day during recess, this boy chased me around the playground trying to hit me on the butt. It was the craziest thing going from boys not being able to talk to me (which was the rule in my old school) to now running from them to keep them away. I don't know where the teacher was, but either I managed to get away or he got distracted by something else. Whatever the case, he did not catch me. Because I felt like no one was there to defend me, this incident left an imprint in my mind that caused me to be afraid to speak up if someone bothered me.

I completed third grade in Chicago and thought we were going to stay there. To my surprise, we went back to Michigan, as my mom and dad had reconciled. We moved into a duplex in Detroit and were re-enrolled in our former school.

My dad used to attend the mosque affiliated with our school, but now he joined a new mosque and attended regularly. Women were not allowed at this mosque, so he and my brother were the only ones in the family who attended. It became apparent that my dad had fully embraced Islam, with a greater commitment than we had initially thought. This time, he expected his family to demonstrate a more significant commitment as well. My mother willfully submitted and encouraged us to do the same, and as children, we did not object. Because everything was separate as far as women were concerned, I saw this as one more way in which I was not accepted. I was still unclear as to how women were supposed to practice any of these standards. I remember my mom saying to me, "You practice in your heart." Somehow, that wasn't enough to stop me from having the repeated conversation of "Why?"

A Missing Link

The internal conversations continued but remained unspoken. Although there were strong principles and disciplines that we as a family was following, something was missing. I was a very good student and loved helping my mother around the house. I would always start dinner while my mother was at work, and I continued to do all the things that girls do in the fourth and fifth grade, except play with Barbie dolls, because I did not like them. I was a very crafty girl and loved to make things. Looking back, the thing I was missing was acceptance.

> *If you ever thought growing up that you were missing something and could not quite put your finger on it, it was probably related to being accepted. While my parents provided a very nurturing environment and in turn, this helped me to have healthy self-esteem, there was a greater acceptance that I was seeking, which was spiritual acceptance.*

Dialogue for Digging In!

1. When you think about acceptance, what is the first thing that comes to mind?
2. How have you dealt with being accepted (or not accepted) by other people?
3. Do you care whether or not you are accepted?
4. Will you keep going whether you are accepted or not?
5. How do you define acceptance?

Chapter Three

M - Meaning

> "For everything that happens in life –
> There is a season, a right time for
> everything under heaven:
> …A time to search."
>
> Ecclesiastes 3:1, 6 (VOICE)

In *Man's Search for Meaning*, Viktor Frankl defines "meaning" beautifully: "A man's deepest desire is to find meaning, and if he can find it, he can survive anything." Frankl was a prisoner in a Nazi concentration camp, and from his experiences, he created the psychotherapeutic technique called "logotherapy." He used this technique (which is based on the theory that the search for a life purpose motivates human nature) to help people overcome depression. He turned pain into purpose. Not even being a Nazi prisoner stopped him from thriving because he found meaning and purpose in his suffering.

My Search for Meaning

During my sixth-grade year, my granddad (my mom's dad) became very ill. When he went to the hospital, we found out that he had a progressive form of pancreatic cancer, and he passed shortly after my twelfth birthday. My dad drove the entire family to Chicago during the most dangerous snowstorm of that winter. I remember the roads being terrible, and we even went off the road. Through all of the snow and accidents on the highway, we still made it safely.

The winter drives were always brutal when we would travel to Chicago, but the weather did not stop us from going. We always went for Thanksgiving and Christmas, either by car or bus, and this drive was no different, except that we were going for my granddad's funeral service. I had so many thoughts, primarily because he was so young.

The funeral service was on a Saturday. All of the younger kids stayed at my grandparent's house, but I was able to go because I was older (and besides, I wanted to go). I do not remember much about my granddads funeral service, but I do remember the songs that were sung, and one specific Scripture reading. This Scripture was the 23rd Psalm. As the reader began to read, I listened intently, **"The Lord is my shepherd; I shall not want. He maketh me to lie down in green pastures: He leadeth me beside the still waters. He restoreth my soul: He leadeth me in the paths of righteousness for His name's sake. Yea, though I walk through the valley of the shadow of death, I will fear no evil: for thou are with me; thy rod and thy staff comfort me. Thou preparest a table before me in the presence of mine enemies: thou anointest my head with oil; my cup runneth over. Surely goodness and mercy shall follow me all the days of my life: and I will dwell in the house of the Lord forever"** (KJV).

This was my granddad's favorite Scripture, and I remember thinking that I had never heard anything like it before. I do not recall the person who read it, but I definitely recall what they read. As I listened, I remember thinking, "The Lord is my shepherd? How can the Lord be a shepherd?"

None of what I heard made any sense to me, but I wanted to know more about these words and this shepherd. I carried this question in my heart for more than ten years, until I eventually got my answer. I was in search of meaning, and I did not even realize it.

We returned home that Sunday evening, and I went to school on Monday. The remainder of the school year was different for me. I missed my granddad but did not express it outwardly. I wondered about his sickness and not understanding the nature of his cancer; I had some unanswered questions. Because of this experience, when someone tells me they have a loved one who has pancreatic cancer, I get a flashback of my granddad. Thankfully, so much has changed for the better, with early detection, medicine, and treatment.

The Switch – Phase 3

We moved over the summer, and even though it was into a historic neighborhood, my parents did not enroll us in our former school, nor did they want us to go to the public school in our neighborhood.

This would have been our first time going to public school, but my parents decided to homeschool us. I was now in the seventh grade; my brother was in fourth grade and my sister was in first grade. My parents did not teach us; instead, they hired a teacher. I have to admit, I missed going to school. What an adjustment!

During this time, my dad hooked up with some people in the neighborhood, and he was introduced to drugs — the "silent killer" of many families. He began to go down a road that would eventually cause him to lose his family. The first year in our new home, I did not notice anything different. My dad continued to go to the mosque, and my brother would go with him. During this time, my brother began learning how to read Arabic. The mosque had a class for the boys —

again, girls were not allowed. If I wanted to learn, either my dad or my brother had to teach me. With my brother having a more defined connection with our religion growing up, it has continued to be a choice for him throughout his life.

By the end of my seventh-grade school year, my mother had found another school for us to attend. It was private, but not religion-based. We did have to wear a uniform, but I did not have to cover my hair. I was going into the eighth grade; my brother was going into fifth, and my sister was going into the second.

A Season of Sadness

I liked this new school, even though my dad was no longer as involved with us. My mom took us to school on her way to work, and picked us up after school. We had a brown station wagon that my uncle gave to my mom. It was a stick shift, and every time she would pick us up, she would have to add water to it or do something under the hood to get it to start. I remember thinking to myself, "Why in the world does the car have to stall every time she picks us up?" Our car rides home seemed to take the longest time, and we always had a feeling of uncertainty, not knowing what to expect when we got home. By this time, my dad was heavily involved in drugs, and he had become physically abusive toward my mom. Toward the middle of the school year, things got progressively worse. I could never have imagined the violence that would be a part of our lives as a result of my dad's drug use. Even though I knew it was because of the drugs, it was still hard to understand how he could get so violent. To this day, I have a hard time with slamming doors and loud voices.

Even though things at home were very hostile, I graduated from the eighth grade as salutatorian. I should have been valedictorian, but they wanted the class president (who was a boy) to give the first speech.

Every year, my mom would send me and my sister to Chicago for the summer to stay with my grandma. My brother did not usually go with us because he was able to be with my dad during the day while my mom was at work. This time, she wanted us all to go, because she knew she needed to leave for good. My brother did not want to leave, and my mom did not force him to go with us. I knew things were going to change (and not for the better) while we were gone. I never knew everything that happened during the year she sent us off, but I do know it was a very dark time for my mother.

I would have never imagined I would be back in Chicago just five years after the first time that my parents separated. This time, I knew more and saw more. It amazes me how many times we had to adjust to what I now understand to be a toxic marriage. I never knew what to expect, and just when I would think that things could not get any worse, something would happen. I was still in search of meaning. And now I was about to go to high school.

Dialogue for Digging In!

1. When you think of "meaning," what is the first thing that comes to your mind?
2. Describe what gives you meaning.
3. When you think of "purpose," what is the first thing that comes to your mind?
4. Do you think meaning and purpose are the same?
5. What about happiness? Do you think it is more important to have happiness or meaning in life?

PART II
The Learning Conversation

"You have to expect things of yourself
before you can do them."

~ Michael Jordan

These next three chapters are going to cover the second stage of my transformation. As it relates to the butterfly, this is the "caterpillar stage." During this stage, the caterpillar spends all of its time eating and growing. What you feed on is essential during this stage.

The caterpillar stage for me was where my **learning conversation** occurred. The key components during this stage for me were *gaining confidence*, *being optimistic*, and *understanding my beliefs and purpose*.

Chapter Four

C - *Confidence*

> "For everything that happens in life —
> There is a season, a right time for
> everything under heaven:
> …A time to plant."
>
> Ecclesiastes 3:1-2 (VOICE)

When you think about *confidence*, what is the first thing that comes to your mind? For me, the first thing that comes to mind is *security*. I asked my fourteen-year-old daughter what the first thing that came to her mind was and she said, "Girls." I asked, "Why girls?" She said, "Because girls need to be more confident." She is so right! To be confident means you are full of conviction and certainty. Going from such a traumatic eighth-grade school year to entering high school, my confidence was so low. I did not know what to expect in a new city, especially at this age. Even though I had some experience being in Chicago, this time it was different. My mother and brother were in Michigan, while my sister and I were in Chicago. My family was separated again.

The Switch – Phase 4

Often, the absence of a parent leaves a void. As a fourteen-year-old, I had no idea what a "parental void" looked like. I knew that my mother was in danger and needed to leave, and I did not care how it happened — I just wanted her to be safe. My entire first year of high school came with so many changes, and I did not know what the future held for my family. I knew that my mom was looking to get transferred to Chicago, but that was all I knew.

A Father Wound

As a child, you are supposed to be nurtured by two loving parents. The absence of this love from either one of your parents can have many consequences. The absence of love from your birth father creates what we call a "father wound," which can occur even if your father was at home while you were growing up. The wound can be caused by neglect (not having your emotional and physical needs met), divorce, separation, death, abuse, control, and withholding love and affection. My father wound occurred primarily because of my parents' divorce and the absence of affirmation from my father as a teen. I received them as a young girl, but from about the time I entered the seventh grade on, I do not recall any affection from my father. Without hearing "I love you" or "I'm proud of you" from my father as a teenage girl, I found myself vulnerable and withdrawn at times, and I did not feel much protected.

New Beginnings

During this year of separation, several things happened, both good and bad. I was now going to high school in Chicago. I actually had to take the bus to get there (this was not a neighborhood high school), and not a yellow school bus —

I had to take public transportation. A good thing for me was that the school that I chose was the same one that my neighbor went to, so I was able to go with her and she showed me the ropes. I met a lot of people at school, even though I was new. I also had a few cousins who went there as well.

The first quarter, I got excellent grades. I wanted to try out for the softball team but my grandma would not let me, because I would be coming home late by myself. I did not do any extra-curricular activities as a freshman, or at any other time while in high school. I also remember that at the school's attendance assembly (you were invited if you had perfect attendance) I won a framed Michael Jordan poster. I had to go up on the stage to receive it and I was wearing a Detroit Piston's championship t-shirt. It was hilarious. The emcee joked with me about taking the poster back (she didn't). After that, everyone knew me as the "Detroit Girl."

My Confidence Shaken

I was adjusting to being in high school, and dealing with the fact that my mom and brother were still in Michigan. Things were going well, until one afternoon when I came home from school, and my cousin was over at my grandma's house. We were talking in the kitchen, and then he told me to come in the front room to watch television.

I followed him to the living room, and in a moment's time he pushed me onto the couch...and molested me right in my grandma's living room. My whole world changed in the blink of an eye. I do not even know how it happened, because it was so fast. After it happened though, I withdrew and became very nervous around him.

This was actually not the first time that it happened (but it *was* the last time) — I just did not fully remember because I was younger the first time. It took several years before I said anything about what happened, and unfortunately, when I did say something after the second time it happened, I was treated as if I was the cause. There was no acknowledgement that it even happened. The only thing I remember being said about it was why I continued to be around him at different family functions. No one said or did anything that I was aware of.

When you get responses like that, it sometimes makes you question what happened, even when you *know* it happened. You think "Am I crazy or something?" At the time, I did not know anything about forgiveness. I only knew how to bury things and somehow believe that it would disappear. While burying and hiding worked sometimes, the memory could resurface if I heard someone say something about him or even mention his name. It was tough to handle, and my confidence in speaking up was shattered.

> *44% of sexual assault victims are under the age of 18. If you have ever been sexually violated and have not told anyone, it is not too late to do so (Stamoulis, K).*

The Switch – Phase 5

At the end of the school year, I was all set for the summer. I was ready for my mother and brother to move to Chicago, and find a place for us to live. News Flash! We were moving, but it was not anywhere in Chicago. My mom told me that my sister and I would be moving back to Michigan. She had found a really nice townhome, and gotten a promotion at work. I had serious mixed feelings about this change. I was so fragile on the inside, but on the outside, everything seemed to be okay.

I badly wanted to have some normalcy. I did not realize at the time that moving me and my sister back to Michigan was the best thing my mom could have done for us. We were going to be moving to some suburb I had never heard of called Southfield. I cried the whole ride back. In our new neighborhood, there were hardly any sidewalks to walk on. I was used to walking everywhere on a sidewalk or taking the bus. There was no real bus system — everyone had cars in the suburbs. I was not the least bit excited about this. I really did not care that I would have my own room and closet space — the bottom line was that I was moving again…and I did *not like it*.

Reconnecting

Now that we were back together, we were adjusting to a single family home. We all had to adjust to being together again, and even though that part was not hard, we had to get through the outcome of my parents' divorce. It was funny because we all just picked up and kept going. However, I still had these internal conversations going on as my coping mechanism for my pain. I was entering my second year of high school; my brother was going into seventh grade, and my sister was going into the third grade. Because all of our schools were neighborhood schools, all of the kids grew up together. This was a benefit for my brother and sister because we stayed in Southfield for the remainder of all of our schooling. For me, however, entering the tenth grade was very challenging because I did not know anyone. High school is a little different when it comes to making friends and fitting in. You have all of the various "groups." Because I enrolled late, my math and science classes were with juniors, so a lot of people thought I was a junior.

Regaining Confidence

I met people quickly, but I still was not happy during my first year at this school. I missed my friends in Chicago, and it took some time for me to get used to the kids driving and having better cars than what my mom was driving. This was a big adjustment for me. One of the things my mom allowed me to do was work when I turned sixteen. Being able to work helped me with my confidence because I had new responsibilities and gained customer service skills. Working was also helpful because I had money and was able to buy my own clothes.

My senior year was the best. I ran for homecoming queen because I thought it would be fun. I got to walk the homecoming court, participated in the parade, and wore a tiara. Even though I did not win (I knew I would not), I had a lot of fun. I had a surprising thing happen during this year. For spring break, instead of going on the senior trip, I decided I would go back to Chicago and visit my friends and my old high school. During my visit to the school, I wanted to go to the college counselor's office. To my surprise, the office was no comparison to the one at my current school. I remember thinking, "Where are all of the resources? How can you get any help deciding what you want to do when you go to college? Or what if you don't want to go to college?" At my current high school, we had a lot of resources for colleges and trade schools, and the counselors helped us a lot with understanding different majors and finding career options. Because of the resources provided by my high school, I had decided I wanted to be a pharmacist, so that is what I was going to major in for college.

My Belief System

Even though I was doing well in high school, there was something missing. I remember talking to my mom about our religion. By now, my outer appearance showed no evidence that I was a Muslim. She told me that what mattered was what was in my heart. I remember holding on to her words tightly. In my heart, I *believed*; however, I did not have much *understanding*. There were only two of the pillars that I knew I was doing correctly: my belief in God, and fasting. I did not pray five times a day and there was no charity giving because we did not belong to a mosque, nor was there any pilgrimage to Mecca happening anytime soon. (The pilgrimage to Mecca is only required if you are able to go. It is understood that not everyone will be able to do this.)

One of the things I did to gain a better understanding of my faith was to write about Islam for my research and writing class. I did a comparison paper between the Nation of Islam and Orthodox Islam. This paper was like my "stamp of self-approval" for gaining a better understanding of why I believed what I believed. I became very confident in what I believed and I was sure that I was on the right path.

My High School Graduation

It had been four years since I had last seen my dad, but I invited him to attend my high school graduation. He attended, and although I was happy he came, I cannot help but recall how painful it was. We had not talked in years, and the last memories I had were of all of the fights between him and my mother. I could not shake those memories. We continued to stay in contact for my first year of college, but after that first year, it would be several years before I saw him again.

Dialogue for Digging In!

1. How would you rate your level of confidence on a scale from 1 to 10 (with 10 being the highest)?
2. If you gave yourself a score over 8, what are the areas in your life you feel deserved that score?
3. If you gave yourself a score less than 8, why?
4. What makes you feel confident?
5. How can you increase your confidence level?

Challenge!

Try this experiment. Do something bold for a week that you would not normally do, and write down some of your thoughts at the end of the week.

-What "bold" change did you make?

-How did you feel at the beginning of the experiment? Nervous? Afraid? Self-conscious?

-Did anyone notice or comment on the change?

-How did you feel at the end of the experiment? Do you plan to continue with the change? Why or why not?

Some examples of things you could do: start a conversation with a stranger, put on a bold lipstick color, or change the way you wear your hair.

Chapter Five

O - *Optimism*

"Optimism is the faith that leads to achievement.
Nothing can be done without hope and confidence."

~Helen Keller

"For everything that happens in life –
There is a season, a right time for
everything under heaven:
...A time for a warm embrace."

Ecclesiastes 3:1, 5 (VOICE)

To be optimistic means "to be hopeful and confident about the future or the successful outcome of something." One thing I can say is that I was very optimistic about my future. I considered myself very fortunate to have a mother who sacrificed a lot for her children to go to the best schools. Optimistic was the one thing I always tried to be. I had a positive attitude about both good and bad things. Even now, it takes a lot to get me to think any other way but optimistic and positive.

My College Years

After graduating from high school, I decided I would stay at home and commute instead of going away to college. I really wanted to go to Michigan State University (MSU), but when the fees started coming in, plus the fact that I would later have to transfer to a school with a pharmacy program, I decided to stay home and attend Wayne State University (WSU).

My mother let me make all of my college decisions. She never told me not to go to MSU — I just knew that as the first person in my family who was going to college, I had to make some adjustments. This was a turning point in my life, and going to college was a huge accomplishment. I was ready for the journey and I was thankful for my mother's sacrifice to move us back to Michigan and send us to a school in a city that was unfamiliar.

I was accepted into WSU as a pre-pharmacy student. After my second year, I was all set to apply to pharmacy school, so I submitted my application and waited for my acceptance letter to come in the mail. The letter that I received in the mail was not an acceptance letter; to my dismay, it was a rejection letter. The rejection letter came with instructions. One of these instructions was to come to a meeting before the start of the following semester. During this meeting, there was a team of advisors that would coach you through the process of being on a waitlist with the potential of being accepted. This included retaking some classes to score higher grades. There was no guarantee you would be accepted the following year; however, this meeting was a pathway for an opportunity to be accepted.

Making Lemonade

The denial was discouraging, so I ignored the letter and changed my major to biological sciences. To remain optimistic, my rationale for changing my major and graduating with a bachelor's degree in biological sciences was to reapply to pharmacy school with a degree and increase my chances of getting accepted. As it turned out, going to the meeting and following the waitlist process would have probably given me a greater chance of being accepted. This was a big lesson to learn that I did not fully understand until a few years later.

My First "Real" Job

My best friend's mother worked as the director of a pharmacy clinic. I spoke with her about working at her clinic because she knew I wanted to be a pharmacist. When an opening became available, I applied and was hired. During that time, it was a big accomplishment to become certified. I studied for the exam and passed the second time I took it. I did not let the fact that I missed it by a few points the first time stop me from retaking it. That exam was no joke and because I was not in a traditional pharmacy technician program (these programs are primarily offered at trade schools or junior colleges), I had to really study and use all of my on-the-job experience. Because I got such good training working at the clinic, I was able to become certified without doing a pharmacy technician program. (The certification program available for pharmacy technicians is different from the undergraduate courses I was currently taking to get accepted into pharmacy school. These programs were usually offered at trade colleges.)

I worked at the clinic for about three years, and then I worked at a hospital for another three years. It was the best start to this career path. During my tenure at the hospital,

I met a young lady who was transferring to Wayne State and wanted to apply to their pharmacy program. After she applied, she received the same type of letter that I had received a few years prior. I immediately encouraged her to attend the meeting. I used my experience and shared it with anyone going through the process of going to graduate school. I was happy to be able to share my experience with her and tell her to go to the meeting and do whatever they instructed her to do. Today, she is a practicing pharmacist.

The Learning Conversation

Throughout college, I was involved in a long-distance relationship. We were friends in high school, but after we graduated, he went away to school. After our first year of college, he came back home for the summer and we went out a few times. At the end of the summer, we decided to have a committed relationship. As we neared our college graduation, I began to wonder if we would get married, and I asked him what his plans were after college and if he saw our relationship going further. That was a long and difficult conversation, because we both realized that we wanted different things in life. I was not asking to get married the next day — I just wanted to know if he thought it was in our future. Unfortunately, he did not, and we broke up after that conversation.

After we broke up, I was sad, but I knew I needed to focus on my future. I also knew that I needed time to heal, because we were together for four years — pretty much the whole time we were in college. I remember being in my room and having a long conversation with myself as I cried through the pain of an unknown future. Out of this pain, I had my **second pivotal unspoken conversation.** It went as such: "What are you going to do with your life? You thought you were going to be in pharmacy school and now you are not. You will soon be graduating with a degree in biological sciences. You just came out of a long-distance relationship. Now what? What is your purpose in life? What do you really want to do?" At that moment, I decided that after I graduated, I would apply to pharmacy schools in Georgia and Florida (I really wanted to move south), and wherever I got accepted was where I would go. I knew I needed to heal and take time to get to know myself and my purpose. I was filled with expectation as I followed my dream of being a pharmacist. I also decided not to become romantically involved with anyone. I was really excited about exploring, and getting to know this soon-to-be "new me."

Dialogue for Digging In!

1. Do you consider yourself to be optimistic in both good and bad situations? Are you hopeful about your future?

2. Are you flexible enough with your emotions to always believe the good about someone?

3. Do you take responsibility for the things that happen in your life — both good and bad?

4. Do you think that being optimistic takes a special skill? Do you practice being optimistic?

Chapter Six

U - Understanding

"Be the one who nurtures and builds. Be the one who has an understanding and a forgiving heart one who looks for the best in people. Leave people better than you found them."

~Marvin J. Ashton

"For everything that happens in life –
There is a season, a right time for
everything under heaven:
…A time to dance."

Ecclesiastes 3:1, 4 (VOICE)

How do you define love? Usually, we categorize love as a feeling or emotion. I believe that love is an action, and is unconditional. I used to think that love was just an expression of what I did, or how someone treated me, or how they felt about me. We use the word "love" so freely, saying things like, "I love cheesecake," "I love that car," or "I love that color," to the point that we have watered down what love really means. Up until this point in my life, my understanding of love was that it was unconditional. I think we all like to think that we love unconditionally, but if we are really honest with ourselves, this is probably not as true as we would like it to be. We tend to do something because someone has done something for us first. Our love is driven by motive more often than we tend to think it is.

My Dating Experiences

Even though I was raised as a Muslim, I unintentionally only seemed to date men who were Christians. I was not exactly on the "Perfect Wife Selection List" for a Muslim man since I had no outward appearance, such as traditional dress, that would identify me as a Muslim woman. I really did not think about religion when it came to dating and getting married. I thought if you were in love that was all that really mattered, but I sure had a lot to learn about love!) I never thought about the importance of having the same core values about finances, raising children, or other things that come up in a marriage. I looked at other things, such as having similar likes and dislikes. As for the difference in our religious beliefs, I had only two requirements: he could not eat pork or put up a Christmas tree. As long as he followed these two "rules," I was fine with marrying outside of my faith.

For me, most of my foundational beliefs were centered on the customs that I was familiar with. My outer appearance showed no evidence that I was a Muslim, meaning I did not cover my head and I was not practicing any of the other Five Pillars, such as praying five times a day. I was only not eating pork and I would fast during Ramadan. Even still, my heart was completely committed to the ideals and principles of Islam. If you asked me to go to a church, I would not go (although growing up, I went to church often with my aunts). As both a high school and college graduate, you could not have paid me to go to a church.

My Belief System

My understanding of God was that there was indeed only one God, and as long as everyone believed in God, we would see who was right when we all got to heaven. This "understanding" of God seemed conditional too. Many people think that we all believe in the same God, but there is one major difference. Christians believe that Jesus is the Son of God, while Muslims believe that Jesus was one of the prophets of God. Muslims do not believe that Jesus was the Son of God, nor that He is divine or part of a triune God (Islam: Sunni Sect). As long as you say *God,* and not *Jesus* or *Lord,* the assumption is that we are referring to the same God. This is a sure way of "living a life on the wide path of ambiguity."

A New Relationship

Instead of continuing down the path of pursuing my dreams, I found myself reconnecting with a friend that I had not talked to in over a year. Because of my decision to remain single, I had no intention of becoming a couple. Nevertheless, he wooed me. I was unaware that I was still carrying pain from the previous relationship, and even though I knew I did not want to be in a relationship, (especially another long distance one) after three months of him pursuing me, I entered into a relationship with him. His consistency won me over; he was doing the one thing my other boyfriend did not do, which was calling me regularly and making me a priority. In this unhealed, vulnerable state, I found myself maintaining a long-distance relationship with him for over a year. After that year, he proposed to me in October of 1999.

The Engagement

We decided to have a "neutral" wedding ceremony. You may be wondering what exactly a "neutral" wedding ceremony is. Our definition of "neutral" was that the minister would not use the name of Jesus Christ in the ceremony — only God. I can hear you asking, "How do you do this?" Remember, for me, a common misconception was that we all believed in the same God, as long as we are saying *God* and not *Jesus Christ*.

After being adorned with a ring, the planning was pretty much complete. All we needed to do was wait for the date — May 7, 2000. This was going to be my fairy tale. I know it seems like this was a perfect connection. Girl reconnects with boy, boy proposes to girl, girl says yes, they get married…at least, that's how I saw it…and that's what I wanted it to be. There was one problem though (okay, I am sure there were several problems). We did not discuss our core values nor did we discuss my desire to go to pharmacy school. He came to visit, and we talked on the phone, but we neglected to discuss our future. Although we met at Wayne State, he was originally from Chicago, and this meant I would be moving back to Chicago after we got married.

Everything was rosy, and we had a pleasant engagement. I had actually started planning the wedding before he proposed, because we had talked about getting married a couple of times. I had bridal magazines and all other things related to planning a wedding. Who does this? I did! During this time, I had several people around me who were getting married, and I was excited for them. I was even in two weddings during this year. At that point, I had made up my mind that I wanted to be married too. My two closest friends had just gotten married and I was so happy for them. I thought, "I want to be married." In just a short period, I had gone from trying to figure out my life's purpose and what I was going to do after graduation, to being in this fast-paced, long-distance relationship. I was supposed to be moving somewhere warm (preferably Florida or Georgia) and going to pharmacy school. My plans had drastically changed!

The Foundation

Your foundation is very important — both personally and relationally. For me, the fact that my fiancé did not eat pork and did not put up a Christmas tree was not a regular churchgoer, and did not belong to a specific church was okay with me. He was consistent with contacting me and being present, and his intellect reminded me of my dad. I thought we had a solid ground to build a lasting marriage, because we loved each other.

Even though I did not go to church because I was still practicing Islam, and he did not belong to a specific church, I still wanted to do premarital counseling. My two close friends had just gotten married, and I knew they had done counseling, so I wanted to get counseling too. My idea of counseling was to make sure we were on the same page and knew what we wanted for our futures. Because we did not have a mediator to talk us through the important transition we were about to embark upon, we were left doing things on our own. He did not want us to have any counseling, so for me, that meant I was going off of his leading and his suggestions.

We did not talk about our finances and because I was already working, I wanted to make sure I had a job when we got married. I wanted to have security and for me that meant I needed to have a job. I thought it would be good for me to find work in Chicago before we got married. I was working in Michigan as a Pharmacy Technician, and I could have continued at the hospital there, but I did not want to take a chance on not finding work immediately after we got married — I wanted to secure a position before we got married. My fiancé had moved out of his parents' home and was living with two roommates in a townhome, and I moved in with them five months before we were to get married so that I could start working. As I think back, I would have to say that this was not the best decision I could have made. I don't even remember if he asked me to move in with him and his roommates or if I suggested it. All I remember is moving in and going to work. I only moved clothes; all of my other belongings were still at home in Southfield with my mom.

Preparing for the future

With my bachelor's degree, I wanted to continue working in a pharmacy or healthcare setting. I applied for a job at Abbott Laboratories and got through the hiring process, and then the Human Resources Department informed me after validating my undergraduate degree that it had not been completed. This was surprising news, and because I had already moved to Chicago, I had to get approval from my school to take the class at another university and transfer the credits. I got the approval to take the course and my degree was validated after I completed the course.

While I was working on completing the course, I got a job working as a Pharmacy Technician at a home infusion pharmacy. I was not familiar with the suburbs at the time so my daily commute was over two hours round-trip. I did not wait until after we were married to move to Chicago, because I did not feel completely secure about whether my fiancé wanted to fully provide for me. We did not talk about this, and although he helped me with bills prior to us getting married, I did not have full assurance that he actually *wanted* to. I know it sounds weird, but in my gut, this was an area that just did not feel settled. He worked in sales, and I just knew I needed to get a job in Chicago before we got married.

The Wedding Planning

As we were preparing for our wedding day, we needed a minister to marry us. I did not go to church, he did not belong to a church, and we were getting married in Michigan, because that was where the majority of my family lived. I remember asking my two closest friends if their moms would be willing to marry us, and they both lovingly told me no, that because of our different beliefs, there was no way they would be able to perform the ceremony. I completely understood. Today if this were to happen, I would stop and think about it, but at the time, I just knew I wanted to get married. I knew we were *supposed* to get married. Besides, we had already started paying for things — the mansion and reception hall were already secured.

I eventually found someone who would marry us. He was a licensed minister and he worked with my mother. He kept calling us the "Jones" all throughout the ceremony because he did not know us, and he did not have any counseling sessions with us either. It's not that funny now, but at the time, I thought it was. What is even funnier is that I had a traditional wedding but I was not a Christian. I was able to justify getting married because my fiancé did not eat pork, did not put up a Christmas tree for Christmas, and he agreed to have a neutral wedding. After the date was set, the mansion was booked for the ceremony, the hall picked out for the reception, the invitations and wedding colors solidified, and the wedding vows written (I wrote our wedding vows) — we were ready to walk down the aisle. I was getting married!

> *I am sure you are probably wondering about the details of our wedding venue. We were married at the Fisher Mansion in Detroit. It was a Spanish mission-style estate with a mix of vintage Hollywood and Italian Renaissance décor, surrounded by the Detroit River. The main feature of the mansion were the peacocks. They apparently lived on the premises and were "part" of our wedding ceremony, as they kept interrupting with loud singing. Everyone thought it was funny. I really wanted to be outside for the ceremony, but because of the time of year, there was no guarantee with the weather, so we planned to be indoors.*

You might also be wondering why I wrote our wedding vows. I wondered the same thing at the time. I asked him to write his vows, and I would write mine. I remember looking through one of my bridal magazines, and I read this beautiful arrangement of words that were perfect for our wedding vows. I added some things to them, and shared what I wrote with my fiancé. He liked them and did not add anything to them, so I pulled out my wedding checklist and checked off the vows.

The Wedding Day

Our wedding was beautiful. Everything was perfect: the bridesmaid's dresses, the flowers…everything. The only problem on the day of the wedding was that the florist forgot one of the bridesmaid's bouquets, and we ended up using an artificial arrangement from our dressing room that matched the other flowers perfectly. You would have never known one was not like the others, so when I say everything was perfect, everything was *perfect*, down to the flowers. The reception was a lot of fun — everyone danced and had a good time. All of our guests told us that they had the best time celebrating with us.

The Honeymoon

For our honeymoon, we were gifted with a seven-day hotel stay plus airfare to the Dominican Republic. We had a good time and really enjoyed ourselves, but by about day five we were ready to go home. You may be thinking, "You wanted to go home?" Well, that was a bit of a situation…my *husband* was ready to go home. I soon discovered that he was not a real vacation person, and he also did not like being outside that much. This girl loves *all things* outside! Loves vacations, loves exploring, and loves excursions — the list goes on and on. (And yes, I am using the word *love* here!) So, after spending our seven days, we left our tropical paradise, and returned home for the first time as husband and wife.

> *Couples today spend a lot of time planning for the wedding and not enough time making sure they have a solid foundation.*

My lack of understanding of my own belief system allowed me to marry someone who did not have the same faith as I did. My sustainability was not strong because I did not have a solid foundation where my faith was concerned. How in the world could I know someone else's belief system was not strong when my own wasn't strong either? My understanding and acceptance of "multiple ways to the pearly gates," so to speak, put me in a relationship that would not be able to be strong based on my understanding of love, God, and myself. A foundation based on this type of understanding makes you wonder if it is solid enough to withstand the highs and lows of marriage. Only time will tell!

Dialogue for Digging In!

1. When you think about love, what is your understanding of the "concept" of love?
2. I want to challenge you to take note of your core values and belief system and write them down.
3. If you are single and not dating anyone, have you planned your wedding already? Are you content with your singlehood status? If you are not content, what are some things you can do to become content? I would recommend spending some time focusing on contentment.
4. If you are single and engaged, did you plan your wedding before you were engaged?

PART III
The Surviving Conversation

"The feat of surviving is directly related to the capacity of the survivor."

~ **Claire Cameron**

These next four chapters are going to cover the third stage of my transformation. As it relates to the butterfly, this is the *cocoon stage*. During this stage, metamorphosis is taking place. Here, you are at a resting stage, and all of the food you ate in the caterpillar stage is supposed to sustain you during the cocoon stage.

The cocoon stage for me was where my **surviving conversation** occurred. The critical components during this stage for me were *gaining resilience, beauty for ashes, developing gratitude*, and *becoming empowered*.

Chapter Seven

R - Resilience

> "For everything that happens in life –
> There is a season, a right time for
> everything under heaven:
> …A time to bind together."
>
> Ecclesiastes 3:1, 7 (VOICE)

I thought I had an understanding of God, love, and who I was, but everything I had gleaned from my beginning and learning conversations was about to be tested during my cocoon stage. Did I feed on enough of the proper food to sustain me through this next season of life?

The New Mr. and Mrs.

Here I was ten years later, back in Chicago, starting a new life in a city that I considered myself to be very familiar with. However, this was not as easy as I thought it would be. Because I was a family person, we agreed I would be able to go back to Michigan to visit my family regularly. I did visit a few times the first year, however, after that it became challenging. I often found myself going alone because he did not want to travel with me. After having such a beautiful wedding, a tropical honeymoon, and moving into a nice apartment, I was surprised to have so many issues in the beginning months of our marriage.

Our First Home

Our first home was a two-bedroom apartment on the third floor. The neighborhood was nice — I did not know much about the Chicago south suburbs so to me it was fine. I was still working at the home infusion pharmacy in Arlington Heights, so my commute was long but not as long as before.

Our first argument occurred three months after we were married. We were going to his nephew's birthday party, but he stayed out all night the night before. He told me he was coming home, and then told me he was not. The next day, he came back and he had his friend with him. I remember telling him that I did not sign up for him to stay out all night and be so disrespectful. He told me (this became the repeated response to these arguments), "You know where I am." Eventually, with this always being his response, I stopped confronting him about his all-night hangouts. However, I was slowly shutting down, and my inner dialogue would become more common for me.

My most significant unspoken conversation during this first year came after this first argument. I thought to myself, "What in the world am I doing here? I want to go home." I had no friends, and all of his friends were around him. Although I had family in Illinois, only one of my cousins and one of my aunts were close to where I lived. I still felt very alone. Another thing I discovered as I was getting to know him was that he wanted to be a rapper and produce music. Huge newsflash for me! I knew he rapped "for fun" and I was okay with that in the beginning, but I had no idea the level at which he wanted to rap and produce music. His desire to be an entertainer became a big issue moving forward in our marriage because he would provide financial resources to any of the projects that he and his friends were working on; paying for studio time, photo shoots — whatever was needed, he would provide for them. I watched him become more and more eager to provide for those projects without hesitation, yet if I needed something, I dare not ask or I had better have a good reason for it. Because I worked, I found myself providing anything extra I needed outside of the day-to-day household needs.

No Longer Honeymooning

I had not befriended any of our neighbors, but my husband had. I remember coming home from work one day and he was hanging out in the living room with some of them. One of them commented on someone having an affair, and my husband told him not to say anything like that around me because I would not let that person come around. He was right — I had a zero tolerance for "cheating and beating." During their visit, this same neighbor invited us to a couple's party.

My husband accepted the invitation. While at the party, I remember laughing at one of the jokes that were told. I had no idea that it was going to turn into a big deal. Later, I could not even remember the joke. I just thought it was funny and not a big deal. Wrong! For him, it *was* a big deal. He was so angry with me. I remember hiding from him when we got home. He went to the bathroom, and I hid in a closet because I was so scared. I remember hearing him say under his breath, "Where did that broad go?" I thought to myself, "Oh no! If he is calling me 'broad', what the heck is he going to do when I come out of this closet?"

I eventually came out of the closet and asked him why did he call me out of my name? He said, "Because I thought you left." I clearly had no idea how bad his temper was. All I did was laugh at a joke that I now could not even remember. You might be thinking, "At least he did not call you the "b" word!" Well, he did use a "b" word and it was not "beautiful!" This very intense moment left such an impression on me that I began to build a wall, and started walking on eggshells. At that time, I did not even know what "walking on eggshells" really meant. I had no idea that I had just entered what was about to be a long journey of abusive behavior.

A Season of Hurt

After this incident, I became very withdrawn. I did not realize this at the time, but this was where I began to suppress my voice even more. In the beginning, when we would argue I would defend myself. He was very good at arguing his point and confronting me. I hated to argue and I especially did not like confrontations, so I began to shut down, and keep my tears and hurts inside. I was learning to bury my pain.

Another one of my hurts during this first year concerned me applying to pharmacy school. I was studying to take the pharmacy entrance exam. I had scheduled my test for the Fall of 2000 and was all set to take it. I wanted to take a test drive to make sure I knew how to get to the test site, because it was in Evanston, and I had no clue where Evanston was at the time. I did not have the opportunity to take my test drive like I wanted to, because I wanted my husband to go with me and he did not think I needed it. I accepted his reason and figured I would be fine on the day of the test.

I am sure you can guess how that Saturday morning went. I got lost. Not a little lost — I got *big time* lost. Remember, I was still learning my way around Chicago driving to different areas, and at that time there was no GPS — only MapQuest print-out maps and the telephone. I did have a cell phone so I was able to call the testing site, and although the man at the site tried his best to guide me there, I was not successful and missed the exam.

I was so discouraged by not being able to take the test I instantly had a flashback to my denial letter from pharmacy school. I remember sitting in my truck, just crying. I got myself together and went back home. I received no support or encouraging words to try again and reschedule the test from my husband. Again, I buried the pain and continued to go to work at the home infusion pharmacy. I was at a crossroads in my life and wanted to know what I was supposed to do as it related to my career choice. I knew I did not want to be a Pharmacy Technician for all of my life.

Reconnecting with my Dad

Although my dad did not attend our wedding, I reached out to him afterwards during the fall of 2000. He had hurt his back badly while working and I wanted to see how he was doing. During his recovery, my mom let him stay with her (my brother and sister were still living at home). This was a turn of events for our family. My mom had forgiven my dad and was able to help him during his recovery time. Because I was gone by this time, I was not around to experience the connection that was reestablished between my parents, nor was I able to see the impact this had on my brother and sister. There was a lot of healing and mending that needed to occur among all of us.

Becoming Resilient

I really had no idea how much of a shell I had formed to protect myself during this first year, and being able to remain resilient was no small task. For me, resilience came not because I *wanted to,* so I could bounce back from unanticipated marital challenges, but because I *had to,* in order to survive. I quickly learned that the man I thought I knew was quite different now that we were married. Actually, I don't think he was any different — I did not see him functioning in his world until after we were married. Even though I had lived with him for those few months, this was totally different. I felt like I had entered the twilight zone. Even so, I managed to push through the challenges and developed a tough skin.

Celebrating Our First Anniversary

Despite the challenges, it seemed as if a year went by very quickly. There were several moments of learning how to be married and learning how to communicate. We celebrated our one year anniversary at the John Hancock, and when we got home, we ate our wedding cake. Because I had picked such a wonderful bakery for our wedding cake (remember, I did a lot of planning on every detail, including making sure the cake was unforgettable), the top tier one-year frozen cake tasted amazing! It was as if it was just baked. How could things be so bad, when the celebratory cake was so good!

Dialogue for Digging In!

1. When you run into obstacles, road-blocks, or conflicts in your relationships (marriage or other), what is your immediate reaction? Do you get angry? Call a friend or family member? Blame the other person? Or do you look for ways to solve the problem and move forward?

2. If you are married, how would you describe your long-term view over the next five, ten, twenty years?

3. What do you think it means to have a Christ-centered marriage?

4. Men and women have different communication styles. Have you found ways to work through the challenges of these differing styles?

5. How has your relationship changed since you got married? How does it differ from the relationship you shared before the wedding?

Chapter Eight

A - Ashes

"Of one thing, I am perfectly sure. God's story does not end with ashes."

~Elisabeth Elliot

"For everything that happens in life –
There is a season, a right time for
everything under heaven:
…A time to cry."

Ecclesiastes 3:1, 4 (VOICE)

I hate to be a "cupcake smasher," but this part of my journey is going to get a little raw. I want you to think about ashes in the sense of something being destroyed. In this case, it is something literally trying to send you to dust, trying to kill you.

Going into our second year of marriage was "interesting." I was now twenty-six. If you saw us together at family events, you would never have imagined that we argued the whole way there. You also would have never known that I was broken on the inside. By now, I had begun to think that I could not measure up to other women. My husband would invariably make comments about how his friends all dated women who were models or very attractive. In the back of my mind, I would think I was not enough for him like he was looking for more or something else. He had even told me once that he prayed that he would not be tempted to cheat. I remember, thinking, "Why do you need to pray that? Hello! We're married!"

I had *zero* tolerance for cheating, so this was a little shocking that he would say this. I was very naïve when it came to things like fidelity. I assumed that when you make a choice to get married, you honor your marriage! Cheating just never crossed my mind, even with all of the challenges that we were facing.

Our First Move

In May of 2001, we were given the opportunity to move into a four-bedroom, Cape Cod home in the south suburbs. I was excited about this, and thought having a house would be nice. For our first home experience, I was hoping to be able to pick it out together, but we did not get to pick the house. A family friend of my husband just told us, "I have a home. Do you want to rent it with the option to purchase after a year?" We agreed, and moved in July of 2001. The house needed a lot of work: new landscaping, new carpet, new boiler, and new kitchen cabinets. The family friend did minor rehab work, and the rest we did on our own over the course of a few years. I really like home improvement projects so this was fun. My dad even came to town to help with some of the work. We eventually replaced the carpet, put down laminate flooring, updated the landscaping, and updated the kitchen cabinets (this was by far my most favorite because I love to cook, so having an updated kitchen was exciting). The only thing that did not get updated was the boiler.

Going Back to School

Things seemed to be going pretty smoothly, and we were settling into our first home. In April of 2002, the home infusion pharmacy where I was working closed and I needed to find another job. My husband was now enrolled in a master's program to become a certified teacher. He was able to work as a teacher while completing this program. I began looking for work at different hospitals and pharmaceutical companies, and in June of 2002, I started working at a pharmaceutical company that held contracts at different hospitals. I was placed at an inpatient hospital pharmacy in the Chicagoland area. This time, I was not a pharmacy technician; I was now working as a project manager on the business side of the pharmacy.

One of the things I wanted to do as a child was to open a health clinic. Even though I was not going to be going to pharmacy school, I still knew I needed to go back to school. My earlier dreams were to become a pharmacist and get my MBA (Masters of Business Administration) so I could have my own pharmacy. In the fall of 2002, I went to an open house for graduate school. I took my transcripts with me, although I had no idea that they would be doing on-the-spot acceptance if you had specific documents. One of the required documents was college transcripts.

I listened to the presentation about the school and the programs they were offering and decided to apply. This was a win-win. Not only did I have my transcripts with me, but I knew I still wanted to get my MBA even though I was not a pharmacist. My boss told me that with my master's, I was now considered a "super tech" (that was his term for me). He was very excited that I was going to getting my MBA and told me that it would give me many great opportunities and advantages.

Encountering the Ashes

I was happy to be back in school and doing something that was part of a dream I had, but my husband was not that excited about me being in school. He was also in school and thought that I was "competing" with him by going back to school. He would make rude comments about things like me "getting a business degree and not knowing how to balance a checkbook." From our day-to-day interactions, I did not realize that I was in an abusive marriage. I had no physical scars on my face. I was not being pushed down the stairs, nor was I being locked out of my home. I was, however, experiencing relational abuse.

What is Relational Abuse?

Because I was not experiencing the noticeable signs of being physically abused, I did not "qualify" my relationship as being abusive. Relational abuse is "a pattern of abusive and coercive behaviors used to maintain power and control over a former or current intimate partner." It is usually called *intimate relational abuse* or *domestic abuse*. The abuse can be emotional, verbal, financial, sexual, physical, or even spiritual and can include threats, isolation, and intimidation (Fontes, 2015).

The verbal abuse was a little easier for me to recognize. Whenever we would have arguments, his words would cut me deeply. I did not like arguing. I did not have anything to say, and I would just hide on the inside. What I mean is that I would be there physically, but mentally I withdrew. These encounters got so bad that if we were about to go out, he would start an argument with me and I would start crying. By the time we would reach our destination, I was a hot wreck. One time I thought I would be safe because his sister was going with us, but no. He went off on me in front of his sister. This became a norm and his sister would never say anything in my defense.

I Got Your Back, Sis

Everything came full circle for me when my sister came into town to visit us. We were set to go downtown for dancing. On our way downtown, my husband began speeding down the expressway (he had been drinking). We got into an argument (about what I do not know) with my sister in the car.

Now, just so you understand something about my sister; she is a no-nonsense girl and she does not let people talk crazy to her, her family, or anyone else for that matter. So, she's in the back seat and she can hear how our conversation was beginning to get heated. My sister told him, "I don't care what you do when I am not around, but what you are NOT going to do is talk to my sister crazy or any other kind of way in my presence."

Then they got into it, because he thought my sister was not being respectful to him. I will just say this; my sister is my bodyguard even though I am older than she is. That night changed everything! After that, because she stood up to him and challenged him, he never had nice things to say about her. She told me the next day that she did not like what she saw, and that I was not in a safe marriage. She also said the situation reminded her of our past experiences growing up, when our parents began to have violent arguments. This was the first time I had someone who was there to witness us arguing stand up and defend me.

The other abuse I experienced was not easy to identify. I did not know how to acknowledge the sexual abuse. I was married. How could my husband sexually abuse me? That was the million-dollar question.

> **Ladies!** *If you are not in agreement with certain activities inside of the bedroom, and your husband forces you to take part in them anyway, that is considered* **marital (or spousal) rape** *and* **physical abuse.** *Even if you agreed with the act once,* ***it does not authorize the act to continue without asking permission!***

I especially noticed acts of violent sex if my husband was angry with me. I would usually not even know he was upset until he would force me to have sex in unconventional ways.

Some Facts about Marital Rape

When you think about marital rape, you may wonder (like I did) how your husband can "rape" you. For me, because I already had some experience with sexual violence (being molested), I thought that I was imagining things when I would find myself feeling cheap and dirty after we would have sex. The term "marital rape" (or "spousal rape") is used to describe "sexual acts committed without a person's consent or against a person's will by a woman's husband or ex-husband." These acts are usually through physical force, threats of force, or implied harm based on prior assaults. *When a woman submits to sexual acts out of fear or coercion, it is rape.*

Sexual acts include "penile-vaginal intercourse, the insertion of genitals into the mouth or anus, or the insertion of objects into the vagina or anus" (Mahoney, 1998).

Why would a man rape his wife? Again, the million-dollar question. A common myth is that it stems from wives withholding sex. Most often, wives who have been raped by their husbands have also had consensual sexual intercourse. Researchers have found, after speaking with husband-rapists, that they rape to *reinforce their power or control* over their wives or to *express anger* (Tario, 2016). In my case, I knew my husband was doing it for power and control, and he was also expressing anger. These violations continued throughout our marriage.

A Few Categories of Relational Abuse

It took me some time before I was actually able to identify, let alone admit, that I had experienced abuse both as a child, teenager and now as an adult. I believe this was because a common coping mechanism for abuse is to bury it, deny it, and pretend it never happened. Being able to understand the types of relational abuse is helpful. A few categories are physical, verbal, emotional, or sexual. The following are from Leslie Vernick's book, *The Emotionally Destructive Relationship.*

Physical abuse is carried out by hitting, slapping, spitting at, punching, kicking, yanking (hair or limbs), throwing, banging, biting, restraining, or any act of physical coercion or violence directed at another person. The abuser attempts to control and intimidate the victim through violence. They also create an environment of anticipated violence by hitting the wall, raising their fist, or waving a weapon in the air or in your face. *Wherever there is physical abuse, there is always verbal and emotional abuse.*

Verbal and emotional abuse occurs when words and gestures are used to hurt, destroy, control or dominate you. The power of our words is often underestimated. The power of life and death is in your tongue (Proverbs 18:21). The saying, sticks, and stones may break your bones, but words can never hurt you, is by far the biggest lie. Verbal abuse includes name calling, cursing, mocking, criticizing, blaming, devaluing, and manipulating words to deceive or confuse you.

Emotional abuse occurs when you have been degraded, embarrassed, or humiliated in front of family, friends, or coworkers. Emotional abusers undermine the victim to gain control. They usually use a significant target to try and destroy their victim.

Sexual abuse occurs whenever one person forces an unwilling party into having sex or performing sexual acts. Other forms of sexual abuse include pressuring to view or participate in pornography, talking in a derogatory or humiliating way, taking sexually explicit pictures without permission or making uninvited comments. If you have experienced any form of relational abuse, there is a cycle that occurs as well.

The Typical Cycle of Abuse

There are three stages of abuse: green, yellow, and red.

- **Green Stage**: the abuser makes promises, sends flowers, declares love, cries, blames others, enlists family support, or begs for forgiveness. In this stage, both individuals are happy to be in the relationship. During this stage, you usually do not realize you are in an abusive relationship. The abuser at this stage is typically apologetic after becoming irrational and angry over small things. The victim is usually unaware of the abuse because the abuser makes up with some type of gift or affection. This stage is sometimes called the "honeymoon stage."

- **Yellow Stage**: the abuser nitpicks, puts you down, criticizes, intimidates, isolates, destroys property, or withdraws affection. The victim in this stage is nurturing, agreeable, feels tension, walks on eggshells, tries to reason, stays away from others, or tries to appease their partner. During this stage, you usually get into small arguments and the abuser may become frustrated with their partner. This is the longest of the stages and can last anywhere from days to weeks, even years.

- **Red Stage**: the abuser has inflicted sexual and psychological abuse. This can include the use of a weapon, hitting, choking, humiliation, rape, beating, and verbal abuse. In this stage, the victim responds by either leaving, fighting back, trying to reason with the abuser, calling the police, trying to protect themselves, or placating (trying to make them less angry or hostile by "giving in" or making peace with them). This is the shortest and most dangerous stage. This stage is based on one specific incident that leads to an explosion of anger. Some abusers may use a weapon against the victim, pull their hair, or publicly humiliate them.

Rose-Colored Glasses

The cycle of abuse for me was carried out through all three stages: green, yellow, and red. Because of my temperament, and my ability to look for the good in everything, I was walking around with rose-colored glasses on. I had already been walking on eggshells, so the glasses were not easy to spot because people only saw me with a brave face and trying to keep the peace. The key element in the whole cycle that I experienced was *denial*. How could I possibly be in an abusive marriage? I had seen my parents go through this, but that was different because there was actual physical abuse taking place (I had not considered the sexual abuse as abuse). How could this be happening to me? Denial will have you questioning all kinds of things happening to you. Things that you *know are true,* but your mental state has you in clear denial. This may explain why I never felt very secure with him.

My First Response

When I realized that I was being abused, I began to wonder what I could do differently. How could I stop the mistreatment? I also wanted to know how we could find some common ground. Since we did not share the same belief system, I knew something needed to change for this to work. He had begun to challenge me about my belief system, asking me if I even knew what I believed. The biggest thing about his questioning was that it was in an abusive manner. He taunted me with the questions, and it caused me to ask myself this question internally. I secretly thought if I could find out what his belief system was, then maybe this would begin to change our marriage. Perhaps he would not be so angry with me if I could understand where he was coming from. I remember thinking I did not want to end up in a situation like his parents or my parents (fighting all the time or divorced).

Studies on abuse state how most people who are abusers have experienced a form of abuse themselves. I was aware we both came from backgrounds where there was a form of abuse. He shared with me that he wished his parents would have gotten a divorce because the arguing was terrible when he was growing up. I remember thinking how this statement was a huge indicator of his behavior. What was really interesting is that he really did not think our marriage was the same as his parents.

If you are in an abusive relationship and you need help, please go to page 164 for a list of resources to help you.

WARNING! *If you or your children are in immediate danger,* **please call 911.** *Don't wait for the next time, hoping things will get "better." In the case of physical abuse where you or your children are being threatened or harmed, you must remove yourself from the situation and make sure that you are safe before attempting to repair the relationship.*

Dialogue for Digging In!

If you have experienced any type of rape or molestation, here is an opportunity to confront what happened, and release the pain that has been caused by this situation. If you have experienced any other type of abuse such as emotional, verbal, or physical, here is your opportunity to confront that pain as well.

1. Do you fear going home?
2. Is your partner unpredictable?
3. Do you blame yourself for the abuse?
4. Do you feel emotionally numb?
5. Do you think you are alone, helpless, trapped, or isolated?
6. Do you walk on eggshells around your partner?
7. Do you try to keep the peace by doing things you would not normally do?

Chapter Nine

G - Gratitude

"For everything that happens in life –
There is a season, a right time for
everything under heaven:
…A time to tear apart, a time to keep."

Ecclesiastes 3:1, 6 (VOICE)

We had been married a little over two years when we began to talk about having children and decided to start trying. I found out I was pregnant in January 2003, and I was very excited. It was at this moment that I had my **third pivotal inner conversation**. I asked myself how I was going to raise this baby. I had no idea. I was in a marriage that seemed to be a roller coaster ride in nature, and I really just wanted to have a healthy marriage. I asked myself if I could possibly raise this baby the way I was raised, under the same belief system. I also knew that I needed to know what my husband believed as well. Because he would watch church services on television, I would hear different pastors preaching. I remember one day I was listening, and I thought, "Everything he is saying…I believe that." This sparked something in me because I did not even really know what my belief system was. What foundation and legacy could I instill in this baby?

How was I going to be able to empower this baby to use their voice when I felt like my voice was silenced? I had no idea of the shift that was about to happen because of this conversation. **"On the other hand, her childbearing brought about salvation, reversing Eve. But this salvation only comes to those who continue in faith, love, and holiness, gathering it all into maturity. You can depend on this"** (1 Timothy 2:15, MSG).

As I had this vital, life-changing unspoken conversation, I remember standing in front of the mirror in my bedroom one evening. I looked at my belly, grabbed it, and said, "I am having a girl." I was so excited! When I was in the sixth grade, I heard a name that I told myself I would name my daughter when I had one, so, I knew what I wanted to name her. From that moment on, I also knew I had to find the answers to this unspoken conversation. But who was going to answer my questions? And was I ready for the answers?

My Work Situation

Jumping right into marriage after college, I had never quite figured out my purpose. Now, I was a wife and soon-to-be mother. My whole world revolved around this. I did not apply to pharmacy school like I wanted to (although I was working in the healthcare field), and at this point, I was just going through the motions. I enjoyed my work, but I was still missing something.

Midway through my pregnancy, I knew I needed to change positions at work, so I applied for another job within the company and was promoted. With this new role, I was beginning to gain a sense of purpose in my work. There is a balance that comes with working and raising children, and I knew I wanted to do both. I started working at the new hospital in June 2003 when I was six months pregnant. I worked both of the positions for a month until the accounts were closed out.

I thoroughly enjoyed this new hospital. I had a wonderful view of the campus surrounded by trees and all kinds of animals. At lunchtime, I would walk around the buildings. This was perfect, seeing how I liked all things outdoors (except below zero temperatures!). My office was located inside of the conference room where the pharmacy staff would have meetings at and occasionally eat lunch. There was a lady who worked in the pharmacy and she was also active in the women's ministry at her church. She invited me to events often, and she also gave me a copy of *The Purpose Driven Life*. That book, along with the television church programs, began to answer the questions I was having about God, my purpose, and raising my daughter.

The Delivery of My First Baby

I worked up until I could not drive anymore, which was one week before I actually went into labor. The night I was to deliver, I remember taking a shower, because I did not want it to be a false alarm.

My doctor was assigned to Ingalls Memorial Hospital, and that was a long drive, so I wanted to be sure I was in labor. We were supposed to get the "VIP treatment," but that was a laugh. When we finally arrived at the hospital, it was about 1:00 in the morning. They checked me in, and hooked me up to the monitors. I was contracting heavily but was not dilated, so they took the monitors off and then there was a shift change.

The nurse told me that because this was my first pregnancy, I would probably be there for a while. By 3:00 in the morning, the contractions were getting worse and no one came to check on me. Eventually my water broke, and still, no one came in. My mother told me that when your water breaks, the baby will come, and she was correct. They finally came in after my husband alerted them that my water had broken, and when they arrived, the baby was literally about to fall out.

The doctor was upset that I did not have an IV (intravenous needle with the Normal Saline solution to stop dehydration) or any other necessary things in my room to deliver my baby, but everything turned out fine and I delivered a healthy seven-pound, fourteen-ounce baby girl.

My Decision of a Lifetime

I had finally gotten to the place where everything I thought I knew about my belief system was being questioned. The things I would do to find peace and keep the peace in my home just were not working, and now I had this baby girl. It was time for me to come face-to-face with my belief system. I remember holding her in my arms in the hospital and saying to her, "I am going to make this right." When we were released from the hospital and back at home, I remember having this unspoken conversation, "How do I do this? What do I do now?" I remember saying, "I believe in my heart that Jesus Christ is the Son of God." At that moment, nothing changed. No one knew what I had just done. I continued with my unspoken conversations, even about my conversion, but not for long. I remember when I finally told my husband that I believed Jesus Christ was my Lord and Savior, he responded with, "Good. Congratulations."

This did not bother me. I started out thinking I was getting saved because of my family. I found out almost instantly that my salvation was for *me* and *my eternal life*, and all those around me benefited because of the decision that I made to follow Jesus for the rest of my life. I was so happy because my first thoughts were that we now believed the same thing. We could pray together, find a church to attend, and stop all these disagreements. And no more abuse. We were finally going to be in unison, and work out our differences in a healthy way, because I now knew differently. I knew the power of redemption and restoration. I had had a Damascus experience and for me, there was no turning back.

If you openly declare that Jesus is Lord and believe in your heart that God raised him from the dead, you will be saved. **"For it is by believing in your heart that you are made right with God, and it is by openly declaring your faith that you are saved"** (Romans 10:9-10, NLT).

After My Damascus Experience

I took his Bible and began reading and studying it. I also got a copy of the *Power of a Praying Wife* by Stormie Omartian. This book was so helpful! The first chapter starts with *you* changing. Honestly, that really wasn't that hard for me because internally, I knew I could only change myself. Thus, I began my secret journey of changing myself. I just *knew* that the moment that I decided to change, things would start to get better. **"This means that anyone who belongs to Christ has become a new person. The old life is gone; a new life has begun"** (2 Corinthians 5:17, NLT).

I returned to work right before Christmas of 2003, after ten weeks of maternity leave. It was hard to do — but I did it. My daughter stayed with my mother-in-law from the time I went back to work at ten weeks postpartum until she was six months old. After she turned six months, my aunt came from Michigan to stay with us and helped me for six months until she turned one. That was the best thing ever! We were both grateful that my aunt came to help out. Because she was living with us, we did not have as many arguments. I remember my aunt telling me that she thought that how I handled situations with him was smart. For example, we needed to purchase a deep freezer, and I found one at the store. I needed him to meet me at the store to help me get it, but when I called him, he told me he was "busy," and I would have to come home and go back when he was ready. Instead of doing that, I had the people at the store help me get it in the car and brought it home without him coming to help me. When I arrived at the house, I told him the freezer was in the truck. Whenever I needed him to help me with something, his response was usually "that will have to wait," and "it is not a priority." Remember, the one thing that he did to win me over before we were married was to make me and my needs a priority, however, this was clearly no longer the case.

The highlights of a baby's first year are all of the milestones, and the first birthday party or at least these were the highlights for me. With my aunt being with me at home, she was a big help with planning the party. At the time, my daughter was into Elmo, so I wanted the theme to be Elmo. We drove to a Meijer's in Indiana trying to find Elmo-themed cupcake papers. I called before going and they assured me that they had them in stock. The funny thing was when we got there, they did not have them, so I made an Elmo-shaped cake instead. I had no idea that I was starting a trend of making character cakes at least for the next four birthdays! I am forever grateful for my aunt sacrificing that time to come and help me. I still had no idea what I was living through, because I was still wearing those *beautiful* rose-colored glasses.

My daughter had character birthday parties up until she was four years old. For her fifth birthday, we took her to Legoland, which had just opened up in Schaumburg. I remember thinking how weird it felt not having a party for her. At this time, the arguing had really escalated and I had decided not to throw her a party, because inviting people over was going to be a lot of emotional strength that I did not have. I was disappointed about this because I really enjoyed celebrating her birthday.

Finding a Church

For a little while, we went to church with my mother-in-law. She would pick us up on Sundays, and we would go to a Lutheran Church right in the neighborhood. She was a member there. This is the same church she took my husband to when he was a child. We also visited his sister's church for Christmas and Easter in 2004. During this time, I also began going to life group meetings at my aunt's house, which was very close to my home at the time.

By Easter of 2005, we finally began the journey of looking for a church home together, or so I thought. We attended Easter service at Family Harvest Church. This was the church my aunt attended and the life group meetings were part of this church. We continued to go on Sundays; not every Sunday, but more frequently than before. We sat in the back with the families who had small children. I did not mind this, but I would usually be distracted because I either had to take my daughter to the restroom or she wanted to color. They had a children's ministry, but my husband did not want to put her in the classroom.

It was two years of on-again, off-again, but I continued going. By 2007, I was going by myself. I would put my daughter in Children's Church so that I could hear the sermon. The first few times she cried, but I stayed consistent. My aunt told me to just keep taking her, because she would get used to it and would be okay. I did and within a couple of weeks, she stopped crying when I would drop her off. One day when I dropped her off, the worker asked me if I wanted to volunteer to come in and help, and I said okay. I had no idea that I would one day serve as a teacher in this classroom!

Work Relationships

Now that I was a believer in Christ, my lunch conversations with the lady who gave me *The Purpose Driven Life* were a lot more focused on God. I did not know it at the time but she was helping me with my new spiritual walk. I asked her questions and she would always share things with me about God. I worked at this hospital for three years. In December of 2006, the assignment ended, and I needed to look for another job.

I was back to, "What do I really want to do?" I knew that I wanted to do more and the company did not have any open positions that they could transfer me to. An old colleague knew that I was looking for a new job, so she contacted me and let me know that another hospital was looking to start a similar program, and asked me if I was interested in meeting with the director. I said "Yes!" I was only out of work for one month — I began working at the new hospital in January of 2007.

After I met with the director of the pharmacy and the Chief Operating Officer (COO), I told them what I would be able to do for them and what salary I was looking to make. They rewrote the job description, changed the title, and offered me more money. I would be their new Program Coordinator for Patient Assistance Programs.

My New Job

During the orientation, the hospital chaplain came over the intercom and told everyone to take a break so that we could have Morning Prayer. I thought, "This is awesome!" I knew I was in the right place! During my time at this hospital, I was there one year and during this year, I was able to connect with two individuals who would significantly help me over the next year.

When my boss had to deliver the news to me that my position was being eliminated because of the budget, he came to my office with referrals and job recommendations. He told me to take time to look, and go on interviews. When I accepted the news graciously, he said to me that he had never seen anyone respond the way that I responded to being laid off. I told him that I trusted God and was not concerned. I had never had a boss who gave me contacts, and let me have paid time off to go interview.

Dialogue for Digging In!

1. What relationships are you most grateful for?
2. What are you thankful for that you learned about yourself within the past six months?
3. What insights have you gained that you are grateful for?
4. What are you most grateful for that brings beauty to your daily life?
5. What book are you most grateful for and why?
6. What challenging experience has changed your life for the better?

Chapter Ten

E - Empowered

> "For everything that happens in life –
> There is a season, a right time for
> everything under heaven:
> ...A time to go to war, a time to make peace."
>
> Ecclesiastes 3:1, 8 (VOICE)

Now that I was learning more about God and developing my relationship with Him, my unspoken conversations became a dialogue with Him. I had an assurance that I was being heard and I knew how to receive answers...by going to the Word of God.

A Season of Change

Although I trusted God with everything going on, February 2008 was one of my most challenging months. I had a miscarriage, lost my job, and my maternal grandmother was in the hospital, fighting for her life. Talk about emotional! I was beyond emotional! The time off from work was much needed at this point. During this time of experiencing so many losses at once, I was back questioning what I really wanted to do. I thought to myself, "I just want to take this time and worship God." I had been going to church, but I wanted more. I wanted more with my relationship with God. I was so ready to just spend all of my time with Him. I knew after being at the hospital, and working in the healthcare field for all of my adult working life, I wasn't sure of what I wanted to do with this experience.

I knew I had gone as far as I could with these types of program implementations and projects. I was a little unsatisfied and wanted more. I had finished graduate school, and wanted to see what I could do with this new set of skills and education. Even with having an MBA, I still wanted to take time to hear what God wanted me to do; actually, I was still searching for purpose. I had found my Father, and now I needed to know what He wanted me to do. I wanted to work for Him. Even though being in the marketplace, I was working for Him — I still wanted more. I found myself having the same conversations that I had when I finished my undergraduate degree. I asked myself, "What are you going to do now?" I just wanted to know what God wanted me to do. You see, for the longest time, I wanted to be a pharmacist, have my own clinic, and be married with kids. At this time, all I wanted was to go deeper in my relationship with God. It's so funny; I can see now how God has been calling for me my whole life. **"For I know the plans I have for you declares the Lord, plans to prosper you and not to harm you, plans to give you hope and a future" (Jeremiah 29:11, KJV).**

My Season of Worship

I said when I left my job in February 2008 that I was going to spend my time seeking God, and asking Him what my purpose was. The one thing I knew was that I was excited, because now I had more time to spend with God. At this time, the membership class for the church were offered via video, so I signed up to become a member of Family Harvest Church. I completed the class during the summer of 2008. I went to midweek service in the morning. I enjoyed the morning midweek service because it was intimate, and I really got personal time with the pastors. I also volunteered at the church.

Being able to be home and go deeper in God made me really happy, and I began to see how my family was going to be ok now. I thought that whenever my husband and I would have arguments (I use "arguments" because these were more than just disagreements), we would be able to pray about it and come together better. I had so many thoughts about how our marriage could now begin to get strong, because Jesus was now the center.

My family was the reason, or shall I say the cause, of me seeking God. Once I got it though, I realized my salvation was personal. We are all called to walk out our own salvation with ***"fear and trembling"* (Philippians 2:12, NIV, emphasis mine).** The next thing I was ready to do was for us to renew our wedding vows. If you recall, we had the perfect wedding, but the foundation was not built on the Rock, Jesus. I wanted Jesus at the center and I wanted to make my marital covenant with Jesus at the center. I wanted Him acknowledged publicly. This was our fresh start. My husband said we should do it for our ten-year anniversary, but that was two years away. I needed to do this like ASAP. It is interesting that I was the only one who thought there was an urgency for us to renew our vows. If you remember, I wrote our original wedding vows. When I thought about this, it was shocking to me, and made me wonder about his limited involvement in the planning of our wedding. He later told me that he did not want a wedding; he wanted to go to City Hall.

I mentioned I had a miscarriage in February of 2008. We decided to try again and I became pregnant. It appeared that the pregnancy was going along well. During this time,

I wanted to be baptized to declare my decision to follow Jesus publicly. When I made the decision to be baptized, my husband still questioned me about my beliefs. I thought, "This is weird. Why am I still defending what I believe? I thought we were on the same team now! I thought you believed! Why are you questioning me about wanting to get baptized?" He even asked me if I knew what getting baptized meant. I felt like I had to give him a dissertation or something for now believing that Jesus died for me. On June 8, 2008, I got baptized. I was so excited because I was pregnant, and I remember thinking this was so cool that my unborn baby was baptized with me.

After my baptism, we went out for dinner. It was the strangest thing; my husband hardly said anything to me on the ride to the restaurant. I remember him telling his sister that he had a lot of work to do and really should be at home doing it. I had offered to help, but he stated that I could not help him. I was not going to be able to help him with the things he needed to get done. We left the restaurant and rode home in silence.

A few weeks later, I was scheduled for my first prenatal visit. Because I had had a miscarriage in February of that year, my doctor wanted to monitor me closely. My visit was at the hospital instead of at her clinic. I was excited about the visit but I was also a little nervous. It was a longer visit than normal, and after doing the ultrasound, she came back with the results and they were not good. There was no heartbeat. These were the same results as the first miscarriage. I remember being very sad. She told me my options and I decided to let the termination process occur naturally at home. What this means is that I would let the placenta release itself.

It took about a week before this process started. I remember being at home, and my father-in-law came to get my daughter while it happened. My husband had joined a band in April, and on this particular night they had practice, so he went to band practice instead of staying home with me. Initially, I thought to myself, "Wow! He won't even stay home with me to make sure I am okay." I am so thankful that I knew how to talk to God now because He totally took care of me that evening. This time, I was able to reflect on things going on.

When I went in for my checkup after the second miscarriage, my doctor explained to me that stress did not cause the miscarriage. She said sometimes, the egg and sperm don't connect properly (and are not compatible) to allow the fetus to grow, and this was the case for us. In my case, this happened twice. My husband blamed me for the miscarriages, even though my doctor told both of us it wasn't anyone's fault.

My First Church Conference

Two weeks after I had the miscarriage, I was ready for my church's annual conference, which was held in July of 2008. I decided to attend church as often as I could (beyond just Sundays) during the season of me not working. I was not sure how long I was going to be off of work, so I wanted to take advantage of this time. I went the entire week of the conference, and because I was not working, I was able to go to all the sessions both morning and evening. During the conference, I sowed a seed and was in faith for a harvest to receive a new consulting contract.

About a week after I sowed the seed, I received an email from my old COO asking me if I was interested in a consulting project to set up his hospital's patient access program in North Carolina. It would be a weeklong assignment; they would fly me out, cover lodging, and give me a rental car. The hourly rate of the contract was the exact amount of the seed I sowed during the conference. The agreement was effortless. I went in, did the job, and they were pleased. Now, this sounds like a joyous time to celebrate. After all, I was still unemployed and was approaching the end of my unemployment benefits cycle. The beautiful thing about this contract was that I wanted to do consulting work, and I saw this as the perfect opportunity to perhaps officially start my own consulting business. Here is where things got a little interesting.

A Change in Career Paths

I was not the only one who was looking for a career change. At the beginning of the year, before I was laid off, my husband decided that he no longer wanted to teach and that he wanted to pursue real estate. He had been teaching now for about five years. He talked to me about his decision before he resigned and even though I told him I had some concerns about this decision, especially seeing how I was not working, he assured me that everything was going to be okay.

He quit his teaching job and cashed out his retirement to pursue his dream of selling real estate and flipping houses. He had a friend at the time who was heavily involved with flipping houses, and he thought this was the perfect time to make such a big change. We had a small child, I was laid off from work, and he wanted to start a new career path. I thought to myself, "Lord if this is what You want for this family, I trust You."

I am not going to say that I was jumping up and down with excitement about this. It is not that I did not want him to pursue his dreams. The problem was that we had not thoroughly discussed him pursuing real estate full-time and leaving his day job. Because he decided to cash out his retirement, he said that money would cover our living expenses. Unfortunately, the money did not come until about three or four months after the request was made. This decision was made during the Great Recession of 2008 — a time when the economy had taken a turn for the worst. Things were so tight during those months. Because we really never had a plan for our finances, I did not know how to talk to him about our bills or other things concerning our finances.

Finances were always an issue. It was like the TV show episode of *Everybody Hates Chris*, where the mother would have to juggle the money to pay the bills because there was not enough to cover them. She would split the light bill and water bill and make the minimum payments so everything would get a payment. That was how I handled the bill paying — stretching to make sure things were covered. It was ironic that we both had master's degrees but somehow could not come to an agreement about our finances.

It was always so hard, and I could never figure out what the problem was. Because of the financial strain, I took out a personal loan with a high-interest rate to get some relief. Let's just say this was not a good idea. At the time, I did not know what to do, because I needed money and there was not a lot coming in. I did not tell my husband that I had taken out the loan. I finally got the courage to say to him I had taken out a loan during the time I got the news about my contract. (You can probably guess where this is going.) This was the second time I had taken out a loan without him knowing. The first time I took out a loan was for the same reason — things were tight, and I did not know how to ask him for money. It is interesting because the same thing I experienced at the beginning of our marriage — not feeling secure with him — had surfaced both times I took out those loans.

The first time it happened, he threatened to divorce me if I ever did it again. You can only imagine how scared I was to tell him that I had taken out another loan. I honestly thought I would be able to pay it back, and everything would be fine, but everything was not fine. I remember asking God to help me tell him. I do not even remember how much it was (I believe it was $500). He went off in a way that I had never seen before. It was crazy. He even accused me of stealing from him.

My New Contract

I was getting ready to leave for North Carolina for my assignment. Before leaving, I was thinking about how I was going to have time to spend with my Father and read the Word. I was so excited to spend the week worshipping God while completing this assignment.

I was going to be gone for a week and was going to miss my daughter. It was my first time traveling without her. As my husband dropped me off at the airport, he did not even give me any money. Remember, I was not working, and my unemployment benefits were over, so I traveled with no money. Who lets their wife leave town with no money? The company provided me with a rental car, but I could not pick it up because I did not have a credit card or bank card to cover it. I was literally in North Carolina, bankrupt. My sister-in-law sent me one hundred dollars for the week, and I used that money for my cab rides. I was able to schedule the same driver all week. My sister-in-law (not the one who never defended me during our arguments) told my husband that she sent me money, and he got so mad that he made me pay her back when I got home.

My Week in North Carolina

I had moments to spend time with God, but every night my husband would call and harass me about why I took out that loan and continued to threaten me. I was so distracted, and I felt like I did not do the best job that I could have for my client. I remember talking to my aunt on the phone during this week, and she told me that I had to stay focused on God, His love, and His Word, and not to allow the words that were being spoken to me bother me.

I was so fragile. I could not understand how two believers were having such a hard time forgiving, and all the other things that should have been happening at this point. We argued the entire time I was away, and I remember thinking that I just wanted to get my daughter. He accused me of having an affair and said that was the only reason why I got the contract. I thought to myself, "Cheating is the last thing on my mind!" I thought back to his comment about "praying not to be tempted to cheat." I should have remembered that when we were friends several years prior, he had a girlfriend, and was still trying to pursue me. At the time, it turned me off when he told me he had a girlfriend. I thought to myself, "Boy! You need to leave me alone and go be with your girlfriend." I had no idea the significance of that at the time, nor did I think that adultery would ever creep into our home. I did suspect that he was having an affair, but I did not have any proof, and I was not trying to find any. (He admitted to having multiple affairs six months after I left him. At the time, he texted this information to me, and I responded with "Okay. Thank you for sharing this with me." That was it. That was all I said because at the time I remember thinking, "Why are you telling me this now?" He did not apologize for cheating on me — he only said that he had had affairs. The text said, "Just so you know; I cheated on you." He sent another text sometime later referring to his actions as being a "serial cheater.")

My Return Home

At the end of the week, my client was pleased with the outcome of the project. I scheduled a series of weekly phone calls to continue over the next 60 days. I also created a manual that would assist them with any questions they might have if they could not get hold of me. Before I left, they offered me a position. I wanted to stay with everything in me, but I had to get back to Illinois to get my daughter. I knew when I went back home that leaving was not going to be possible, and I had no peace about going back. I just did not know what else to do.

When I arrived home, I did not know what I was coming home to. At this point, I was not sure if I could even call where I was going "home." There was no exchange of hugs or kisses. I remember getting in the car at the airport waiting lot, and I went completely numb. I hugged and kissed my daughter — I had missed her. If I could have sat in the back with her, I would have, but she was not an infant, so I did not have that as an excuse to sit with her.

My Spiritual Covering

The week I was gone, I realized I was covered in prayer because I was being attacked from all angles spiritually. At this time, I was still unemployed. I knew I enjoyed consulting and was ready to start exploring this as a possible new opportunity. The week I got back, I scheduled an appointment with my district pastor. I did not realize that my aunt had spoken to her to let her know what was going on in my marriage. As soon as I entered her office, she informed me that she was not going to tell me to get a divorce. I was shocked because that was not why I was there! I was there because I needed someone to help me understand what I was reading in the Bible. I wanted so badly to know God more in-depth, all I thought about was Him. I had so many questions because I wanted the dots to connect and I wanted to make sure I understood what I was reading. I left her office with a book by Charles Capps (she said that if I wasn't going to read it, don't take it) and she also told me to read the Book of John.

Having an Islamic background, there were a lot of strongholds that needed to be dismantled, and the main one was seeing Jesus as only a prophet. I knew that He was Lord, but when I read through the Book of John, the Word exploded in my heart, and I did not have to deal with any more thoughts about His Lordship after that.

My heart knew, and my mouth confessed, but my mind seemed to wander back and forth. This was a belief system that needed to be uprooted. The Book of John allowed my mind, spirit, soul, and body to all line up. When I got to **John 14:6, "Jesus said to him, I am the way and the truth and the life. No one comes to the Father except through me,"** I said, "There it is!" This Scripture broke every hindering thought I had, and that thing was uprooted! (I encourage you to go back and read the Book of John as a faith refresher).

My Second Meeting

Eventually, I did discuss my marriage with my district pastor, and when I did, I appreciated her wisdom. I had one focus and one focus only, and that was knowing God more. I was not expecting to talk about my marriage, because I "knew" everything was going to be okay and would work out. During our second meeting, I told her about the abuse and other things going on. She said, when I decided to stand for my marriage, I either needed to be the cruise ship or the rowboat. The cruise ship was not going to be moved by every wave; however, the rowboat would. She also told me, that if he hit me then I needed to leave, and keep myself and my daughter safe. At that moment, I decided to be the immoveable cruise ship. After I met with her the second time, I was empowered and ready to stand. I had God's Word, and I was *set*.

My New Work Opportunity

A month after I completed my consulting assignment in North Carolina, I got in touch with a former boss because I saw an opening in her department. (This was the pharmaceutical company where my contract ended in December 2006). This was another contract, and I had worked at this facility in the past. They knew me, and I had a relationship with the customers. We met for lunch to discuss the role, and also the position I took after the contract ended in 2006. I accepted the position and was rehired with my previous seniority and vacation benefits. This made me an employee with over five years with the company.

I started the role in September of 2008, and I was excited to have consistent work. Even though it was what I was previously doing, this time, they added more responsibilities for me. I was able to lead all of the new hire training, and I was able to travel to different sites to train new employees. I liked being able to travel and train; that was the highlight of the job for me.

I had been working for a couple of months, and things were still crazy at home. Even with me deciding to be the cruise ship, I remained faithful. I had paid the loan back (the company did not charge me all the interest), but when I told my husband that, he did not believe me.

He asked me what I did because "they never waive the interest." I told him that I did not do anything. All I knew was that they only charged me the amount of the loan — no interest. He was still not satisfied and continued to accuse me of stealing from him.

After I came back from North Carolina, I began purposely falling asleep in my daughter's room when I read to her every night. On the nights that I did not sleep in her room, I was terrified to be in my bedroom. One night in October I did sleep in our bedroom, but he had fallen asleeping upstairs, so I felt safe because I thought he would stay up there all night. He did not. When he realized I was asleep in the room, he took a pillow and slammed it against my head so hard that I thought he punched me. I did not even know you could be hit that hard with a pillow. I jumped up, and I tried to run out of the room, but he would not let me. I had to endure several hours of him badgering me. Thank God, he did not force me to have sex with him; that would have been even worse.

On my way to work the next day, I was listening to the radio. At the time, I did not realize that October was National Domestic Violence Month. As I was listening to the program, they were discussing abusive relationships. The host began to read off ten things that were signs you were in an abusive relationship. It was then that my rose-colored glasses fell off of my face. I thought to myself, "I am in an abusive marriage!" I had to *hear* the ten signs for the light bulb to turn on. Now I needed to know what to do. I instantly felt the walls caving in on me. Could I have been that naïve? Remember the cycle of abuse — the biggest issue is *being in denial*. I had had enough of being in denial. Nothing that I was experiencing was normal. We did not have normal arguments, and things needed to change. I remember saying it plainly, "Lord, I am ready for a change."

The Night

I wanted my daughter to experience different things. I knew I did not want her to experience the pain of parents who fought or divorced. I began to notice that when we would argue, she would come into the living room and just stand by me. One day, he told her to go back to her room. From his tone and the way he said it to her, I knew that things were not getting any better anytime soon.

On Tuesday, November 11, 2008, I had gone to work as usual. Around 3:00, I received a phone call from my husband. He told me that he needed me to leave work, and go to Western Union to make his car payment. He was not able to make the payment because he had gotten his license taken for speeding, and could not get it back until his court date. I left work and went and paid this car payment for a car that I was not allowed to drive. After I made the payment,

I had no more money in my account, and I was not getting paid until the end of the week.

I left Western Union and went home. I was in the kitchen cooking dinner, and he came in from the backyard. We had a garden and he was bringing in the last of the vegetables. As soon as he put the vegetables in the sink, he began to start up about the money from the loan. He continued to tell me that I had stolen from him and he wanted his money, when I had just finished paying his car note! He told me to call my mother and have her give it to him. At that moment, I told him no, that I was *not* calling my mother and asking her to give him anything. The moment I said no, he went off and slapped everything I was holding out of my hands. At that moment, the only thing I remember was grabbing the phone to call the police. He threw his shoes and hit me with them. Then he asked me why I had the phone. I said, "Because I am about to call the police." I also told him, "This time you put your hands on me, but it is the last time you will ever touch me again." At the time, my daughter was in the living room and saw everything that was going on.

I took her into the bathroom to get her out of the way. I ran her bath water, put her in the tub, and stayed in there with her. He came into the bathroom to say goodbye to her and left. I never put the phone down. I was so shaken up. I called my best friend and told her what happened. She was trying to help me, but I was a wreck — I really could not comprehend what had just taken place. I then called my aunt, and she asked me if I was leaving, or if she was going to have to come and get me.

I was thinking, "Leave? Did what I think just happened really happen?" The one thing I knew was that I did not want him to touch me sexually when he got home, because it was not going to be good, so with my daughter in her pajamas, I put some things in my truck and I left. That was the last time I would be in that house. It took him three days before he called me. He did not try to come to my aunt's, and he did not ask me to come home. His only comment was that I "took his daughter from him."

I never in a million years thought I would have to decide to leave, especially not because of abuse. When I think about this part of my journey and the surviving conversations that took place, I see how my beginning and learning conversations were vital during this season. Had I not kept seeking for answers, I am not sure I would have made it out. Not just out of an abusive marriage, but also out of a religious belief system that was not working for me.

The Next Day

I did not go to work the day after I left. I took my daughter to school, and then I went to the police station to file a report. I remember being very afraid, and shocked that I was at the police station. I told the officer what happened, and he gave me a copy of the report and told me to go to court and file an order of protection.

As I was filling out the report to file the petition, I could not stop crying. I really did not believe I was filing for an order of protection. That day, I was granted an emergency order of protection, and I received a court date to return. At that time, my husband would be there.

When it was time to go to court, I took my aunt with me, and he brought his dad. We were both able to tell what happened on the night of the occurrence, and after we were finished, the judge granted me a one-year order of protection. The order allowed him to pick up our daughter at my aunt's house. Because of the verbal and emotional impact of my husband's communication with me, he could only communicate with me via phone or text per the order, and any other contact required someone else to be present. It was at this moment that the boundary was established — it would be only a few times that we would have verbal conversations. The majority of our communication was through text messages or an occasional email. While the order protected me in one regard, it also helped in keeping my voice silenced.

"Fight and Flight"

In the survival stage of transformation, when we feel threatened, we are prompted with different corrective actions to take. For example, if you saw a glass cylinder about to fall from a building and hit you in the head, you would move quickly to protect yourself. This instinct ensures we get out of danger by way of the "fight, flight or freeze" response. For me, the order of protection was my "fight and flight" response to a harmful situation. I went from finding silence in a noisy world (freeze response) to making the hardest decision I had ever made to leave an abusive marriage (flight response). I chose life.

Dialogue for Digging In!

1. Did you grow up in an abusive home? (Any form of abuse)
2. Are you currently experiencing any abuse in your current relationship?
3. If yes, have you reached out for help?
4. Are you ever afraid to go to sleep at night?

PART IV
The Thriving Conversation

"My mission in life is not merely to survive, but to thrive; and to do so with some passion, some compassion, some humor, and some style."

~ **Maya Angelou**

These final three chapters are going to cover the fourth stage of my transformation. As it relates to the butterfly, this is the *adult stage*. During this stage, the wings of the butterfly are getting strong, so it can take off and fly. If the butterfly tries to fly too soon without fully developing its wings, it can die instantly. It is imperative for the butterfly to know its wings have reached full maturity before leaving the cocoon stage. There is no sure way of knowing when you have reached full maturity until you decide to spread your wings and fly.

The adult stage for me was where my **thriving conversation** occurred. The key components during this stage for me were *overcoming challenges, developing unwavering faith, and becoming stable.*

Chapter Eleven

O – *Overcoming*

> "For everything that happens in life –
> There is a season, a right time for
> everything under heaven:
> …A time for keeping your distance."
>
> **(Ecclesiastes 3:1, 5 VOICE)**

This last part of my transformation was by far the most impactful. I had gone through three stages of unspoken conversations: "beginning," "learning," and "surviving." We have now come to the "thriving" conversation. Every unspoken conversation I ever had brought me to this point. It took massive amounts of courage to step out of the boat. I am who I am because of what I went through. I was ready for pruning and preparation for what was coming next.

Most often, when we tend to stay in survival mode, it is possible to toggle between the "learning and surviving" and never quite reach the "thriving." We may think we are thriving, but we are merely surviving. There is nothing wrong with surviving, although I realized that while I was escaping, I was not effectively looking after myself. I was too busy taking care of everyone around me. It took me a long time to realize that while surviving is necessary, thriving is best. The first thing I needed to do to begin to jump past just surviving was to overcome some setbacks.

The Separation

It was now March, four months after I had left my husband on that cold November night. I was staying with my aunt and had not filed for divorce. I don't know whether I was waiting for my husband to do something — change or whatever — but I was waiting. One evening, he called and asked if I would consider going to counseling. I thought this was a trick question, because while we were together I suggested we go to counseling, and he said no. Initially, I wanted to say no, but before I could, I was led to respond with an okay. I then said, "You have to find the counselor though." He agreed, and a few days later he called to tell me that he found a counselor at a neighborhood church by our old house, where he was still living. We arranged the time for our session and met the following week for our first session. I was not sure what to expect, but I went.

When I arrived at the church, he was already there. We sat down, and the first thing the counselor asked us was why we were there. My husband said that he was there to save his marriage, and I said that I was there for understanding. The counselor responded by saying that we both wanted the same thing — it just was worded differently. I internally agreed with her, because I did not want to get divorced. I wanted us to work out what was going on and begin to build our foundation on God's Word with Jesus as the center, but this was going to take some real digging.

My question was, "Were we going to engage in the digging and uprooting process or were we going to point fingers and assign blame?"

The Counseling Sessions

As the first session proceeded, we were both able to share what we wanted to share, based on some questions that the counselor asked us to help us articulate our feelings. My husband shared first, and then I talked. I remember it as being the first time I was able to speak and be heard. I knew that this session was a moment where being vulnerable would have to be a choice for me. I had to know that I was in a safe place and having the counselor helped with this a little. I still had walls up, but I listened to what my husband shared. At the end of the session, our counselor gave us homework. We were to read Ephesians 4:31-32 and answer a series of questions to prepare for our next meeting, which we scheduled for the following week.

One week passed, and it was time for our second session. On my way there, I remember asking God to watch over me and that if He wanted me to continue with the sessions, to please make it clear. It was an honest, quiet conversation that I had with Him as I was driving to the session. I really wanted to allow God to soften me, and heal the hurt that I was still experiencing from the years of abuse.

During the first session, I did not even get to talk about the abuse. This time, I was able to go first. Now that it was my turn I shared, answered questions, cried, and managed to express a lot of the pain that I experienced through the years.

Overall, the session was going well. My husband spoke after me, and then the time came for us to set the next appointment. Because the session was really intense, I wanted to take a little more time between meetings. I suggested that we meet in a week-and-a-half, but he wanted to meet sooner. I remember the timeframe not being that much of a difference, but he did not want to come on the day I had suggested. I said, "We can make it a few days later." At that moment, he rose up out of the seat and went completely off.

He screamed at me and answered every question I had asked on my drive over. He told me that it was a waste of time, that I was the cause of everything, and then told me to go ahead and file for divorce because he was done. Then he stormed out.

I could not move. I started crying, and just sat there. The counselor would not let me leave until she knew that he had left the parking lot. She told me that it was not my fault and that if I wanted to talk, I could. I sat for about 30 minutes, and then I left to go to my aunt's house. Because counseling was new for us, I understood the reaction and the outburst from my husband. It took him several days to call me after that night.

While we were talking, his comment to me was, "If I wanted to continue counseling, then he would go back." I remember thinking, "If I wanted to continue? You left, how is this now for me to say, if I want to continue going?"

At that moment, I had to make another difficult decision. I decided during that conversation that I was not going to continue with counseling. There were several reasons for this. The first was that there was no urgency for him to contact me. Every question that I had asked in my car he had answered when he exploded, and he was not willing to sacrifice or fight for me. Everything during these counseling sessions was about him, and what I did to him, and how I broke up our happy family. He also said I was now destroying our daughter's future, and I did not have a father that wanted to be in my life. A month after that last counseling session in March, I filed for divorce.

Beginning Again

The thought that I was getting a divorce was scary. We had been married for over eight years. When I left in November, it had been eight and half years, and I remember having my

fourth pivotal conversation. It really sounded a lot like my second conversation. The difference this time was that I knew *Who* I was talking to, and I knew I was being heard. I said, "What am I going to do? I want to be able to use my gifts and skills for Your Kingdom, God. I want to serve You with my life. I want this season to be different. I am completely surrendered to You, Lord."

A week after having that conversation, I was in church, and in the morning announcements, they said that the church was looking for healthcare professionals to go on an upcoming medical mission trip to Guatemala. I sat there and thought, "Well, I am a healthcare professional, but how can a pharmacy technician be helpful?" I was not a doctor or a dentist. After service, I went to the table to get information, and that is when I met Dr. Phillips and his wife. I told him I was a pharmacy technician and wanted to know if there was a need for my skills, gifts, and talents. He told me "Absolutely," and gave me an application. He told me on this trip I would be a pharmacist. I laughed, and he said, "Don't laugh! You will be the pharmacist."

After our conversation, I submitted the application. I was approved to go, and Dr. Phillips gave me a list of the drugs that we were taking with us. At that moment, everything I ever learned rushed through me! Because I was working in a hospital, I let them know I was going on a medical mission trip and they donated additional supplies such as dispensing bottles, antibiotics, counting trays, and children's multivitamins.

The trip was scheduled for June 2009, for one week. Once we arrived in Guatemala, everyone was taken to their areas. I was taken to the pharmacy area to set up for the dispensing of the medications. It was a small room with a pickup window, and it had a fan to blow the hot air around. I was so excited to be doing what I enjoyed! Because of my strong background in medications, I set the pharmacy up as if it were a Walgreens.

I had a counting area where the medicine was bottled. I even had an area to prepare the liquid antibiotics. Everything was set, down to the Spanish labels with pictures. As I was finishing setting up for the day, I heard a quiet whisper say, "This is your pharmacy." I started crying and said, "Thank you, Lord!"

I had such an amazing time serving the people in Guatemala during that trip. I had such a good time that I went back the following year! When I went the second time, I decided that I did not want to use an interpreter unless I needed one to dispense the medication. I had taken over three semesters of Spanish in college, and because of the efficiency of my labels, I could read them to the patients.

The first year, I was too nervous and did not want to mess up the directions, but for this next trip, I was confident that I would not mess up. Besides, the interpreter would be available if needed. This was one of my best decisions because I was able to interact with the people more. Being ready to go on two mission trips allowed me to be able to focus on God, and not what I was going through; specifically, the divorce.

The Comeback

During this time of overcoming one of the most challenging life experiences that I had faced as an adult, I decided to go back to school. After going on my second mission trip, when I came back, I knew I needed to keep focused on things that would build me up. I was still working in the hospital and was looking to do more, however, I was not sure exactly what "more" was. I had passed the timeframe of going to pharmacy school, and at this point after my mission trips, I was okay with not going to pharmacy school anymore.

I began looking at doctoral programs and was reminded by my friend about the program she was currently completing. At this point, I knew I wanted to continue growing in my relationship with God and the school she attended was a Christian university. Although the doctoral program was not a theological degree, I was still moved by the school's motto, "Education with a Christian purpose." I applied for the program, and completed my interview and in-person writing sample — all I needed to do was wait. Several days after the interview process, I received a phone call from the program director. I still remember his exact words, "Ms. Vinegar, you have been accepted to be in Cohort IV for the Doctor of Education in Ethical Leadership program." I went numb on the phone, but I said thank you as calmly as I could. I hung up the phone, and screamed so loud I'm sure the car behind me heard me!

Changing Career Paths

Starting this doctoral program was one of the most uplifting things I could have done during this season. Often, when we go through setbacks, we tend to have a hard time getting back up. What I did with the monkey wrenches thrown at me was I decided to overcome them. A few months into the program, I was still questioning what I wanted to do next as far as my career options were concerned. I had reached the highest level I could at my company, and although they encouraged professional development and me going back to school, they would only approve my tuition reimbursement if I was getting another master's degree. Still, I did not let that stop me from continuing with my program.

At the time of my annual review, I had high marks in all the key areas. My supervisor had one area of concern, and that was concerning my reimbursement numbers. Even though my position was not a sales position, I had monthly revenue targets to meet. These targets were met by having a specific dollar amount of reimbursement claims from the different pharmaceutical companies. While I met the numbers every month, she knew that I could do more, and I agreed with her. At the end of our meeting, she told me the most freeing thing. She said, "You are really good at what you do. You are in school for your doctorate, and I know you enjoy training and development. You need to decide what you want to do." I remember thinking, "I *do* need to decide what I want to do."

I had already begun looking at jobs at universities and was looking to switch from healthcare to education because I had grown to like training and development. There were also a lot of changes taking place with healthcare, and I was not sure if I wanted to stay in the industry doing what I was currently doing, and I did not want to go back to school for a medical degree. I had finally released myself from the pressure of not going to pharmacy school.

During this time, I began volunteering at my church's Bible college. I helped with the PowerPoints for the video lectures, and I also developed a training manual for the faculty for the learning management system (LMS). As I was applying for positions in the education field, I was told there was a position opening up at the Bible college. I remember asking more details about the position, and then I applied. A few months later, I began working as the LMS Administrator. I was really excited about this new role because I was able to use my background in training and development for the LMS component, and I was also able to use my project management background to help with the school's accreditation process.

Making the decision to go on those mission trips, returning to school, and changing career paths was the best thing for me during this season. When I think about my time of overcoming and preparing for the future, I had one thought: I did not want my daughter to experience growing up in a home that was abusive. I knew what that looked like, and did not want to repeat it. I thought after accepting Jesus as my Lord and Savior that things would begin to change. I just knew they would! I knew it was not going to be overnight though. Remember what I said in my survival stage; the one person you know you can change is *you*. You can only decide to change yourself. If you don't believe you need to change, then you won't. I had come out of a world where I honestly *thought* I was happy. I realize now that it was fake happiness. I was pushing through abuse trying to maintain peace, and no one knew because on the outside everything appeared to be just fine.

Dialogue for Digging In!

1. When you think about overcoming, look at it from the perspective of thriving, not just surviving. What does overcoming look like to you?
2. How do you handle a setback in life?
3. Have you put boundaries in place for your relationships? Look at both work and personal relationships.
4. What do you see yourself doing over the next 12 – 24 months?
5. How often do you criticize yourself?

Chapter Twelve

U - Unwavering

> "For everything that happens in life –
> There is a season, a right time for
> everything under heaven:
> …A time to heal."
>
> (Ecclesiastes 3:1, 3 VOICE)

One of the key things that I have learned about leaving a state of "surviving" and entering a "thriving" mode is that you need to know the difference between the two. You need to understand what surviving looks like, and know when to leave it. For me, this meant developing unwavering faith. To enter fully into this steadfast faith, I had to be very intentional about what I spent my time doing.

A Season of Healing

Having the opportunity to go back to school, along with the rigor of the program, really stretched me beyond how I ever thought I could be stretched. The program was three years long, and what I liked most about it was when I completed all the coursework, my dissertation was also going to be completed. I learned so much about myself, and I met wonderful people. My cohort was considered the closest group that had the most fun. We considered ourselves family. Had I not been in this program while going through my divorce, I am not sure how I would have made it through. My divorce was finalized December of 2010. After what seemed like the longest year-and-a-half of my life, I was now single again.

Now that it was finalized, I was able to fully focus on my daughter, school, and my new career. These areas were significant for my healing. I wanted to make sure that the necessary time was taken to mend. A year after my divorce was final, I found a program for people recovering from divorce called "Divorce Care." There was also a program for children. I signed both myself and my daughter up for the program. This was a 13-week, Biblically-based program for men and women to heal after a separation or divorce. I realized from this program that healing after divorce is a process that should not be rushed. I have never quite understood how someone could go through a divorce and get right into another relationship within a month's timeframe. I knew that I wanted to get married one day again, but I also knew that I was not going to rush into a new relationship.

From Grief to Healing

You may be in the middle of a nasty divorce, are separated from your spouse, or you may be recovering from another kind of trauma. I want to share with you a process for healing. You may be wondering why we are looking at healing from a thriving mode as opposed to a surviving mode. Remember — when you are in survival mode, you are really just trying to *get through* something. You have three responses in survival mode: fight, flight, or freeze. In the thriving mode, you are not doing any of these. You have gotten beyond the trauma recovery and are now walking free. You are seeking wholeness now. I will share both the grieving and healing process for divorce. Both of these processes are similar to other types of trauma.

The grieving process of divorce has seven stages. The stages are *denial, pain and fear, anger, bargaining, guilt, depression,* and *acceptance*. I went through all of these stages during my divorce; however, I also went through some of these in my marriage because of the abuse. I was in a state of denial during my marriage and the divorce. I was also depressed and very fearful. One of the ways I knew I was in denial was because I jumped into doing other things to take my mind off of the divorce. I pushed through all of the stages and reached the acceptance stage after the first court date was set.

- **Denial:** In this stage, you are protecting yourself from being emotionally overwhelmed. This stage acts as a coping mechanism. You may also experience shock and numbness at what has happened. In a sense, you are going through the motions.

- **Pain and Fear:** In this stage, you are getting through the actual hurt that was caused or the broken trust from the relationship. As denial wears off, reality begins to sink in, and you start to feel the pain of the loss and fear about the future.

- **Anger:** During this stage, you are looking for someone to blame. The blame may be toward your ex-spouse, your in-laws, parents, friends, yourself, or even your children. Anger is healthy to a degree. If your feelings seem to be out of control or directed against the wrong people, your children specifically, you should seek professional help. Your ex-spouse and children may also blame you for breaking up the family, and you will have to handle this.

- **Bargaining:** During this stage, you are deciding if you made the right decision to leave. Your emotions are up and down, and you are trying to rationalize if you are going in the right direction with your life.

- **Guilt:** At this stage, it is normal to think about how you could have done things differently or how you could have prevented situations and made your marriage work. Here, you are usually questioning your behavior in the marriage, and you want a "do-over."

- **Depression:** In this stage, you are experiencing a healthy form of depression. When depression hits, it will have you sad the majority of the time. Getting help from an expert is important during this stage. You will want to be able to cry and talk it out with someone who can help you get past the toxic emotions.

- **Acceptance:** This is the "reality check" stage. Here, you have come to terms with what has happened, and you are now moving ahead. You are ready to start your new life. Your regrets are the ones you can live with by not beating yourself up about them or questioning your decisions.

The healing process is the most vital step in the journey. One of the things that I had to do during my healing process was, to be honest with what was happening. Like the grieving process, the healing process has similar stages. They are *survival, anger, seeking and self-development, acceptance and adaptation, forgiving, and thriving*. The healing process allows you to embrace transformation. Here, we are becoming more immovable and unwavering.

Deliverance is a Choice

For you to fully live with purpose, you need to be healed and be whole. Sometimes, your healing looks different than you would expect. This was true for me. One thing I did not realize was that I had created my healing through the survival mode. I had put up walls of protection for myself, and I had buried the pain of the years of abuse. It took a while before I recognized that it was *me* who had barricaded *myself.* I was living in a cocoon created by me. I also realized that God was patient with me as I begin to allow Him access to unpeel the "onion layers." As each layer would come off, I would cry, and keep going. Here is where we often "jump ship," because we do not want to go through the unpeeling process. I have learned that deliverance is a *choice*. Making that choice can be painful, but on the other side of liberation is wholeness and freedom.

A Relentless Pursuit

I looked at my divorce as an opportunity to grow both mentally and spiritually. I approached mental growth by going back to school for my doctorate. Knowing that only two percent of the population holds this level of a degree was a big deal to me. It took steadfastness and unwavering faith to believe such a level of excellence was even possible, especially in the middle of going through a divorce.

My spiritual development became a *non-negotiable, relentless pursuit*. I used my time to study the Word of God and build my faith. I desired to live out Mark 4:14, where the sower sows the word. God's Word also has final authority in my life. *This is it for me*. If I cannot back *what I am saying* and *what I believe* with the Word of God, then I have nothing to say about the matter. The funny thing is, it can be misinterpreted as being too holy or having "Bible breath." The cool thing about studying God's Word is that it teaches you how to engage with people without being "extra." I learned this just by listening to people, and finding out what they had going on. Take the time to listen. Sometimes, we tend to miss this because we are too busy talking. I have learned to be a good, discerning listener.

Walking in Forgiveness and Love

Establishing an unwavering faith has to be accompanied by walking in forgiveness and love. I had to decide to forgive deliberately, and love no matter what had happened to me. I did this by taking a long look back at the situations that God had brought me out of. The first area had to do with my "father wound." The next was being molested as a teenager, and the last was being abused in my marriage. Confronting these incidents were not easy. My relationship with my father has gotten better over the years, and as far as the molestation is concerned, I forgave my cousin years ago. The funny thing about forgiveness is that when you see the person that caused the pain, you may have a flashback to the time when you were hurt. I have learned that does not mean you have not forgiven them. The incident does not go away. However, your desire to get revenge ("Get them Lord!") does eventually go away. These Scriptures are there for this reason: **"Vengeance is *mine*,"** and **"*Pray* for those who mistreat you" (Romans 12:19 and Matthew 5:44, emphasis added).**

The Importance of Forgiveness

Forgiving my ex-husband was something that I had to do before I was even fully aware of what forgiveness meant. To survive an abusive relationship, you tend to forgive by default, however, sometimes you end up either becoming bitter or passive-aggressive. When I began studying Scriptures on forgiveness and love, I knew I needed to watch out for passive-aggressive tendencies. Bitterness sets in when you walk in unforgiveness. Another area to watch out for is "behaving like a victim." Yes, you were mistreated, but the victim mentality occurs the moment you decide to use what happened to you as an excuse not to get back up and keep going.

Victim mentality feeds off of "look what they did to me." One thing I had to do with forgiving my husband was to recognize that I was hurt by him not loving me. When I realized that my heart was broken, I remember sitting in the park one Saturday afternoon. I motioned to my chest as if I was grabbing my heart. I said, "Lord, I am taking my heart out of his hands and I am placing it back in Your hands." When I did this, I felt the broken-heartedness lift off of me. If you believe your heart is in the wrong hands right now, I want to encourage you to release your heart and put it back in your Father's hands. Let's pause at this for a moment!

> *Forgiveness is a PROCESS! Forgiveness is **not** letting the offender off the hook. Forgiveness is **not** the same as reconciliation. Forgiveness is **returning to God the right to take care of justice**. Forgiveness starts with a **decision**.* (Sweet, R. 2000)

Unwavering Faith

Unwavering faith is built on trust. Many people have huge trust issues. I remember when my pastor said, "Trust God, love people (Robb Thompson). That was the best and most delivering thing. I would usually say, "I don't trust them." I had to develop an attitude of full trust when it came to know that my God loves me (Ephesians 3:19 - 20). I also had to know that He cared for my day-to-day needs (Matthew 6:33).

Becoming unwavering in your faith means that you take seriously **"not to be moved by what you are seeing (2 Corinthians 5:7)."** You are just really sure of your God! You revere Him. You worship Him. You glorify His name.

Dialogue for Digging In!

1. What does faith mean to you?
2. Are you wearing an "invisible blindfold" when it comes to walking by sight?
3. Do you have trust issues?
4. Have you put into practice a victim mentality?
5. What are the things you worry about most?

Chapter Thirteen

S - Stable

*"For everything that happens in life –
There is a season, a right time for
everything under heaven:
...A time to collect the harvest."*

(Ecclesiastes 3:1, 2 VOICE)

We have come to the end of our transformation process; however, the transformation is ongoing. We go from glory to glory. It's *line upon line, precept upon precept, here a little, there a little* (2 Corinthians 3:18 and Isaiah 28:10, emphasis added). When we think about thriving, being stable is a key component. A stable person is "one who has a renewed, sane, and sensible mind" (Romans 12:1) and is "not easily upset or disturbed" (Ephesians 3:17 and Colossians 2:7). My stability was not an overnight process, but rather a daily "on purpose" practice for me. During this stage of my transformation, several things took place to help me become secure.

New Season of Adventure

In May of 2013, I completed the Doctor of Education in Ethical Leadership program. This was by far one of the most memorable moments of my life! I remember someone asking me how I did it. How did I work full-time, raise my daughter, and go through such an intense program? My response was, "Only by God's grace, and a determination to finish what I started." *Your tenacity to finish something,* mixed with *God's grace,* equals completion. Even if through the journey things get off track, if you do not give up, you will *always* end up on top! Make up your mind to be a finisher. I learned the key to being a successful finisher is to be led by God, and don't jump in front of Him (Psalm 119:105, Proverbs 19:21, Psalm 32: 8).

After I graduated, I had the opportunity to continue growing in my stability. I say it was an opportunity because had it not happened, it would have probably taken me an extra year to finish my program. Right before I needed to turn in Chapter 3 of my dissertation (November 2012), I was laid off from my position at the Bible college when the decision was made to close the school. Initially, I was sad about it, and then as I sat one morning, reflecting and preparing to finish my chapter, I realized that I was far behind. I remember thinking, "Wow! How was I ever going to finish this dissertation on time?" At that moment, I saw beyond my immediate circumstances.

Open Doors

Some time passed after I had been laid off, (fifteen months to be exact) before I found another job. It was funny how it happened. I had stopped looking for a job for a while, just pressed into God's Word, and I had taken my mind off of the agony of job searching. I kept thinking that this was supposed to be easier, especially with my doctorate. I remember it clearly.

It was a Friday evening, and I sat down on the couch, opened my computer, and only applied to positions where I could upload my resume and cover letter. On Monday, I had three emails requesting an interview, and I had three phone interviews scheduled that week! The following week, I had two in-person interviews. One was in healthcare, and the other was in higher education, which is where I wanted to be. By the third week, the college had contacted me to set up a third interview, and I had not heard back from the healthcare facility. I scheduled the third interview, and that same week, I got a job offer! I accepted it and was working by March 2014. From that Friday evening to my final interview, it took three weeks! While at the college, I received a promotion after 18 months.

The "One-Year-No-Dating" Challenge

Being single again, I had a different perspective on singleness. I know that I want to get married again but I am also perfectly content if I do not (Psalm 131:2 and Philippians 4:12, emphasis added). My focus is to keep my mind set on things above (Colossians 3:2). With this as my guide, my greatest desire is to seek God's Kingdom and His righteousness (Matthew 6:33 and Psalm 27:4).

Having this desire, I was prompted one day in June of 2014 to watch a teaching series by Andy Stanley (Pastor of North Point Community Church) on singleness and dating. During one of the messages, he challenged his single audience members to commit to one year of no dating and to spend that time entirely focused on God. He stated to the audience, "Become the one you would like to marry." After the message ended, I said to the Lord, "Is this something I should do?" At the time, I was not dating anyone, and I did not really have any potential prospects either. But the thought that I wrestled with was, "What if he comes as soon as I make this commitment?" I argued with myself for about 30 minutes on why I should not, and did not, need to do this. Finally, I said, "Yes, Lord. I will make the commitment." I spent so much time focusing on the "buts" and "what-ifs" that I was about to miss something fundamental in my transformation journey. That evening, I wrote out a prayer and signed the commitment not to date, or think about dating or marriage, for a year. I also purchased and read the book *Your Knight in Shining Armor: Discovering Your Lifelong Love* by P. Bunny Wilson, on the recommendation of a friend. It was not just about the dating; it was also about what I was focusing on in my thoughts. What you meditate on is what comes out. **"Where your treasure is, there will your heart be also" (Matthew 6:21).**

That was one of the best things I could have done during this season. We spend so much time talking ourselves out of what God wants from us, either because we are afraid we may miss something, or because we want to remain in control. Had I not made this commitment, I would not have been prepared to recognize a counterfeit relationship. This time firmly rooted my heart in God's love for me. I remember asking Him to show me my new name, and I was led to the Scripture in **Isaiah 61:4: "No longer will they call you deserted, or name your land Desolate. But you will be called Hephzibah, and your land Beulah; for the Lord will take delight in you, and your land will be married."** When I read this, I began to cry because I felt God's love. I was very familiar with Isaiah 54:5 (For your Maker is your husband), but this one specifically resonated because Hephzibah means "my delight is in her." When we **"delight ourselves in the Lord, then He grants us the desires of our hearts" (Psalm 37:4).** My caveat for this promise is that I want *my* desires to be *God's desires* first. The more time you spend in His Word and fellowshipping with Him, the more your desires become His desires.

Total Immersion

During this commitment time, I had decided that this was not just going to be a one-year commitment: it was a lifestyle change. I was not doing this to get married once the year was over, or to be pursued by a godly man.

Before the year was over, my daughter and I traveled to Fort Worth, Texas for our first Southwest Believer's Convention, hosted by Kenneth Copeland Ministries. Because my thoughts were unhindered by marriage and dating, that time away was a total immersion in God's Word. The seed that was planted in my heart that year changed me, and redirected my focus concerning my career path and ministry. Both of our lives were changed that week. This was one of our new vacation spots. I call it our "faithcation." For me, it was like being at Disney World, the "happiest place on earth."

Listen! Can you hear me now?

A big moment for me during this stage of transformation was regaining my voice. I had to come out of hiding and begin to speak. For a long time, I did not have verbal conversations with my ex-husband — everything took place through text messaging for the most part. It was very seldom that we had voice conversations. I had a lot of boundaries set to protect myself after we separated and now that we were divorced. I realize that these boundaries were necessary, however, I hid behind them and did a lot of burying the pain myself. In 2016, I began reading *Beyond Boundaries: Learning to Trust Again in Relationships* by John Townsend. I highly recommend this book. It covers different scenarios to help you determine if you need to re-enter a relationship and how to do it, or if you need to move on from the relationship.

It was not until I watched the movie *The Shack* that the combination of this book and the protective boundaries I put in place made me realize that I had buried my pain and hurt. It was Father's Day of 2017, and I was sitting in the park. I said, "Lord, I have buried this hurt, and did not even know it. I do not even know *where* I buried it. I want to give it all to You, but where is it?" At that moment, I experienced an outpouring of tears as I was delivered. At that moment, I became a "Daddy's girl."

I was gaining strength in an area where I was still fragile, and I was finding the courage to let the walls down. One day, my ex-husband texted me and wanted to pick up our daughter for the weekend. I had never given him my address, but I responded, "Yes, you can pick her up." Just like that. He said "Okay. Thank you." For years, I was afraid to have him pick her up from my house, and in one text message, it was over. I remember saying "That was easy, Lord!" The Scripture came to me, **"Come to me, all you who are weary and burdened and I will give you rest" (Matthew 11:28).** I remember falling into His rest at that moment.

My Spoken Conversation

The next month, I was thinking about how I wanted to celebrate my daughter's birthday. Every year, we split the time, and she would usually have two celebrations.

One of the things I had been praying about was being able to have her sweet sixteen together (at this time, it was two years away). The problem with having one party was that we at least needed to be talking and doing better interactively co-parenting. As the time was getting closer to her birthday, I received a text message suggesting that we all go out for dinner this year. I remember being on a walk with my friend, and I immediately responded (not to him, but out loud), "No, I don't want to do that. We can continue doing birthdays the way we have been. I'm okay if you want to take her out on her actual birthday. I will take her out on the weekend." That was not a big deal for me; I was okay with him spending time with her. I am sure you can guess what happened next.

Handing it Over

After returning home from my walk, I was trying to get my thoughts together. Just as I was typing my response text to say it was okay for him to take her out…blah, blah, blah… my friend in Texas called me on the phone. I told her what happened and she said, "No. You need to go, and trust God." She knew that this was one of those wounds that I had buried, and that God was leading me to hand it over, while my hurt was causing me to hold on and continue protecting myself. I was still functioning in survival mode. To cross over to thriving, I needed to release this and trust God, so I responded with, "Yes, we can go to dinner for her birthday." I again remember thinking, "Well, that was easy, Lord! Easier than the first response I was trying to send!" I am so grateful for "God interruptions!"

We went to dinner, and after, my daughter and I returned home, I remember being so tired. I had worked myself up into such an emotional state that when everything settled, I fell asleep shortly after we got home that evening. I was still getting to the point of being able to trust God when it came to interacting with my ex-husband because the civil part of our relationship was not a constant. There were still moments when he would verbally antagonize me. I can say I still had trust issues and was not sure if this was something that I needed or wanted to do. As it turns out, going to dinner was a more significant release than I knew I needed. When we hold on to our hurt and build walls, and it is time for the walls to come down, it is important to remember that the *Lord is there with you*, helping you knock down the walls of hurt and pain. I had to hand over the shovel that was continuing to keep my hurt buried. God was saying to me, "It is time! Are you ready to thrive?" I then felt more strength in my voice. I was no longer having unspoken conversations!

Dialogue for Digging In!

1. Do you consider yourself to be a stable person?
2. What does stability look like for you?
3. Has there ever been a time when you felt like you were "self-protecting?" What were the circumstances that caused you to go into "protection" mode?
4. Do you have healthy boundaries?
5. Have you buried your pain so deeply that you do not even know where it is hidden?
6. Do you need to release some self-buried pain? If so, take this time to do so.

"Our deepest fear is not that we are inadequate. Our deepest fear is that we are powerful beyond measure. It is our light, not our darkness that most frightens us. We ask ourselves, 'Who am I to be brilliant, gorgeous, talented, fabulous?' Actually, who are you not to be? You are a child of God. You playing small does not serve the world. There is nothing enlightened about shrinking so that other people won't feel insecure around you. We are all meant to shine, as children do. We were born to make manifest the glory of God that is within us. It's not just in some of us; it's in everyone. And as we let our own light shine, we unconsciously give other people permission to do the same. As we are liberated from our own fear, our presence automatically liberates others."

Marianne Williamson

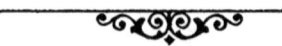

From This Day Forward

Today I have given you the choice between life and death; between blessings and curses. Now I call on heaven and earth to witness the choice you make. Oh, that you would choose life, so that you and your descendants might live!

(Deuteronomy 30:19, NLT)

Today is your day! It's a new season for you! You have journeyed with me through some of the most challenging and rewarding times of my life. You have walked through my take transformation, from an insecure girl to a mature woman of God. I pray that during this journey, you have had time to really reflect, dig up anything that has been holding you back, and hand it over to your Heavenly Father for complete healing and wholeness. Honestly, I am most excited about you reading this part because you have gone with me and hopefully have fully engaged in the Saleh moments, and you have allowed your Heavenly Father to bury your hurts — the ones you thought you gave to Him but picked back up. I do understand that this is not an overnight thing, so give yourself the freedom to take one day at a time. Whatever you do though, *don't give up*!

The most important thing I have learned throughout my journey to restoration is that in the beginning conversations, I was forming an identity and looking to be accepted and find meaning in life. As I entered the learning conversations (my caterpillar stage), I was trying to build my confidence and remain optimistic about the direction my life was heading, and with my career choices. During this stage, I also walked you through my understanding of love, God, and who I was. In the next part of the journey, we entered my survival conversations. This was my "cocoon stage," and some of my most painful experiences occurred during this stage. This is the stage where I was becoming resilient, and also where I went through a season of ashes. A turn of my journey came during my season of gratitude and empowerment.

Finally, we made it to my thriving conversations. This was where transformation fully took place. You walked with me as I overcame a difficult season of going through a divorce. By this time, I was developing unwavering faith, and gaining stability. My sister, we have come a long way together! I hope you have been able to heal and release the buried pain. I want to leave you with a set of Scriptures for each one of my experiences. You can use these Scriptures for daily prayers, or you can do a word study on these topics. I also want to encourage you to make a practice of reading your Bible daily. Whatever you do, do not let a day go by without hearing and reading God's Word. His Word brings life to you. Whatever path that the Lord leads you down to go deeper, follow it with all your heart!

Next Steps

- If you have not made the decision to make Jesus Christ the Lord of your life, I want to give you the opportunity to do that now. You will find a prayer for redemption in Appendix **A**.

- Pray a prayer of restoration. I have a prayer for healing in Appendix **B**.

- Take the "I Am Courageous" challenge. You will find the creed located in Appendix **C**. For 30 days; I want you to say the creed *out loud* in the morning and the evening.

- Finally, color your butterfly wings! There is a picture of a butterfly for you to color, located in Appendix **D**.

Now that we have taken care of these things, below you will find Scriptures to accompany the topics you have just journeyed through with me. You did it! I am so proud of you! Say this with me, "I Am Courageous!"

I – Identity Scriptures

Genesis 1:27: "So God created man in His *own* image; in the image of God He created him; male and female He created them." (NKJV)

A – Acceptance Scriptures

Ephesians 1:5-6: "Having predestinated us unto the adoption of children by Jesus Christ to himself, according to the good pleasure of his will, to the praise of the glory of his grace, wherein he hath made us accepted in the beloved." (KJV)

M – Meaning Scriptures

Jeremiah 29:11: "For I know the plans *and* thoughts that I have for you,' says the Lord, 'plans for peace *and* well-being and not for disaster, to give you a future and a hope." (AMP)

C – Confidence Scriptures

Psalm 27:14: "Wait for *and* confidently expect the Lord; be strong and let your heart take courage; yes, wait for *and* confidently expect the Lord." (AMP)

O – Optimistic Scriptures

Psalm 37:3-5: "Trust in the Lord, and do good; dwell in the land, and feed on His faithfulness. Delight yourself also in the Lord, and He shall give you the desires of your heart. Commit your way to the Lord, trust also in Him, and He shall bring *it* to pass. (NKJV)

U – Understanding Scriptures

Proverbs 3:5-6: "Trust in the Lord with all your heart, and lean not on your own understanding; in all your ways acknowledge Him and he will direct your paths." (MEV)

R – Resilience Scriptures

Ephesians 6:10-18: "And that about wraps it up. God is strong, and he wants you strong. So, take everything the Master has set out for you, well-made weapons of the best materials. And put them to use so you will be able to stand up to everything the Devil throws your way. This is no afternoon athletic contest that we'll walk away from and forget about in a couple of hours. This is for keeps! It's a life-or-death fight to the finish against the Devil and all his angels. Be prepared. You're up against far more than you can handle on your own.

Take all the help you can get, every weapon God has issued, so that when it's all over but the shouting, you'll still be on your feet. Truth, righteousness, peace, faith, and salvation are more than words. Learn how to apply them. You'll need them throughout your life. God's Word is an *indispensable* weapon. In the same way, prayer is essential in this ongoing warfare. Pray hard and long. Pray for your brothers and sisters. Keep your eyes open. Keep each other's spirits up so that no one falls behind or drops out." (MSG)

A – Ashes Scriptures

Isaiah 61:1-7: "The Spirit of God, the Master, is on me because God anointed me. He sent me to preach good news to the poor, heal the heartbroken, announce freedom to all captives, pardon all prisoners. God sent me to announce the year of his grace - a celebration of God's destruction of our enemies - and to comfort all who mourn, to care for the needs of all who mourn in Zion, give them bouquets of roses instead of ashes, messages of joy instead of news of doom, a praising heart instead of a languid spirit. Rename them "Oaks of Righteousness" planted by God to display his glory. They'll rebuild the old ruins, raise a new city out of the wreckage. They'll start over on the ruined cities, take the rubble left behind and make it new. You'll hire outsiders to herd your flocks and foreigners to work your fields, but you'll have the title "Priests of God," honored as ministers of our God. You'll feast on the bounty of nations, you'll bask in their glory. Because you got a double dose of trouble and more than your share of contempt. Your inheritance in the land will be doubled and your joy go on forever." (MSG)

G – Gratitude Scriptures

Colossians 3:15-17: "And let the peace of God rule in your hearts, to which also you were called in one body; and be thankful. Let the word of Christ dwell in you richly in all wisdom, teaching and admonishing one another in psalms and hymns and spiritual songs, singing with grace in your hearts to the Lord. And whatever you do in word or deed, *do all in the name of the Lord Jesus, giving thanks to God the Father through Him.*" (NKJV)

E – Empowerment Scriptures

2 Peter 1:3-4: "His divine power has given to us all things that pertain to life and godliness through the knowledge of Him who has called us by His own glory and excellence, by which He has given to us exceedingly great and precious promises, so that through these things you might become partakers of the divine nature and escape the corruption that is in the world through lust." (MEV)

O – Overcoming Scriptures

1 John 5:3-5: "For this is the love of God, that we keep his commandments: and his commandments are not grievous. For whatsoever is born of God overcometh the world: and this is the victory that overcometh the world, even our faith. Who is he that overcometh the world, but he that believeth that Jesus is the Son of God? (KJV)

Revelation 12:11-12: "And they overcame *and* conquered him because of the blood of the Lamb and because of the word of their testimony, for they did not love their life *and* renounce their faith even when faced with death. Therefore rejoice, O heavens and you who dwell in them [in the presence of God]. Woe to the earth and the sea, because the devil has come down to you in great wrath, knowing that he has *only* a short time [remaining]!" (AMP)

U – Unwavering Scriptures

2 Peter 1:5-9: "So, don't lose a minute in building on what you've been given, complementing your basic faith with good character, spiritual understanding, alert discipline, passionate patience, reverent wonder, warm friendliness, and generous love, each dimension fitting into and developing the others. With these qualities active and growing in your lives, no grass will grow under your feet, no day will pass without its reward as you mature in your experience of our Master Jesus. Without these qualities, you can't see what's right before you, oblivious that your old sinful life has been wiped off the books." (MSG)

S – Stability Scriptures

Proverbs 31:25: "Strength and dignity are her clothing *and* her position is strong and secure; and she smiles at the future [knowing that she and her family are prepared]." (AMP)

Proverbs 31:29-30: "Many women do noble things, but you surpass them all. Charm is deceptive, and beauty is fleeting; but a woman who fears the Lord is to be praised." (NIV)

APPENDICES

Appendix **A**: My Identity – Redemption
Appendix **B**: My Healing – Restoration
Appendix **C**: My Victory – Courageous Creed Challenge
Appendix **D**: My New Wings

Appendix A

My Identity – A Prayer of Redemption

If you have never made Jesus the Lord of your life, I invite you to do so now. Say this prayer out loud: *"No longer do I want to live in fear. Lord, take my life and do something with it. I confess with my mouth that Jesus Christ is Lord and I believe in my heart that God raised Him from the dead. For You said that if anyone who believes in their heart and confesses with their mouth, then they are saved. I receive today my gift of salvation. No more shame, no more guilt, and no more condemnation. For there is now no condemnation for those who are in Christ Jesus. I am a new creature and old things have passed away and all things have become new."* (Scripture references: Romans 10:10-11, Romans 8:1, 2 Corinthians 5:17)

Date of Decision to Commit or Rededicate:

Appendix B

My Healing – A Prayer of Restoration

"*Heavenly Father, You know, and have seen, everything that has happened to me, and You know everything that is in my heart. You know the hurts and the pain. You even know where I buried them. Today, I take back my heart and I place it in Your hands. You are the keeper and protector of my heart. If anyone is looking to have my heart, they will have to receive it from You.*

Now Father, create in me a clean heart and renew a right spirit in me. I am asking you to clean me and make me whole. I am asking to be set free and delivered from all past hurts, pain, and heartaches. I release to you all of these areas, (say the areas) and also the areas that I do not know where I have been hurt and abused. I am asking you to heal and restore me. I walk in love and forgiveness, and I release those who have harmed me.

I surrender my body to you, and recognize that my body is a temple for the Holy Spirit to dwell in. You have purchased me, and I am not my own, for it is in You that I move and have my being. I keep my mind filled with beauty and truth and I meditate on things that are honorable, right, pure, lovely, good, virtuous and praiseworthy.

It is one thing I seek, and one thing I desire, to dwell in the house of the Lord all the days of my life and to behold Your beauty and to enquire in Your temple.

I love You with all my heart, soul, mind, and strength. I enter into Your gates with thanksgiving and into Your courts with praise. I thank You and bless Your Holy name.

Today, I receive my healing. Thank you for restoring me and healing my heart. In Jesus' name, I pray! Amen!" (Scripture references: **Psalm 51:10-12, Ephesians 4:31-32, 1 Corinthians 6:9, Acts 17:28, Philippians 4:8, Psalm 27:4, Mark 12:30-31, Psalm 100:4, Mark 11:23-24**)

Appendix C

My Victory

"I Am Courageous" Creed

My **I**dentity is in Christ
My **A**cceptance is in the Beloved
My **M**eaning is in Christ
My **C**onfidence is in Christ
My **O**ptimism is in Christ
My **U**nderstanding of Love is in Christ
My **R**esilience is in Christ
My **A**shes are now beauty in Christ
My **G**ratitude is in Christ
My **E**mpowerment is in Christ
My **O**vercoming is in Christ
My **U**nwavering faith is in Christ and the Word of God
My **S**tability is in Christ

Appendix D

My New Wings!

Photo credit: openclipart.org

Notes

Introduction – The Butterfly Effect of an Unspoken Conversation

1. The Academy of Natural Sciences of Drexel University, "Butterfly Life Cycle," http://ansp.org/exhibits/online-exhibits/butterflies/lifecycle/
2. Allen, J., "The Butterfly Effect," http://www.blogos.org/keepwatch/christian-life-transformation.php

Chapter One I – Identity

1. Merriam-Webster, *"personality"* https://www.merriam-webster.com/dictionary/personality
2. Merriam-Webster, "identity" https://www.merriam-webster.com/dictionary/idenity
3. Editors of Encyclopedia Britannica, *"Moorish Science Temple of America,"* https://www.britannica.com/topic/Moorish-Science-Temple-of-America
4. *Coming to America*, directed by John Landis (Eddie Murphy Productions, 1988).

5. Well, K. 2016. *"Three Detroit Charter Schools Closing this Year,"* Accessed 11/23/17 http://michiganradio.org/post/three-detroit-charter-schools-closing-year

6. *"Islam: Sunni Sect,"* http://www.jewishvirtuallibrary.org/sunni-islam

7. "Identity Theft Statistics," https://www.javelinstrategy.com/press-release/identity-fraud-hits-all-time-high-167-million-us-victims-2017-according-new-javelin

Chapter Two A-Acceptance

1. Merriam-Webster, *"acceptance,"* https://www.merriam-webster.com/dictionary/acceptance

2. Oxford Islamic Studies Online, *"Pillars of Islam,"* http://www.oxfordislamicstudies.com/article/opr/t125/e1859

Chapter Three M-Meaning

1. Frankl, V. 2006. *Man's Search for Meaning.* Beacon Press, Boston, Massachusetts. www.beacon.org

Chapter Four C-Confidence

1. Merriam-Webster, *"confident,"* https://www.merriam-webster.com/dictionary/confident

2. Davis, A. *"Understanding and Healing the Father Wound,"*

https://www.focusonthefamily.ca/content/
   understanding-and-healing-the-father-wound

3. Stamoulis, K. *"7 Ways to Help a Teen Survivor of Sexual Assault,"* https://www.psychologytoday.com/us/blog/the-new-teen-age/201207/7-ways-help-teen-survivor-sexual-assault

Chapter Five O-Optimism

1. Merriam-Webster, "optimistic," https://www.merriam-webster.com/dictionary/optimistic

2. Encyclopedia of Detroit, *Fisher Mansion*, https://detroithistorical.org/learn/encycloped-ia-of-detroit/fisher-mansion

Chapter Eight A-Ashes

1. Fontes, L. 2015. *"When Relationship Abuse is Hard to Recognize,"* https://www.psychologytoday.com/us/blog/invisible-chains/201508/when-relationship-abuse-is-hard-recognize

2. Mahoney, P. 1998. *"Sexual Assault in Marriage: Prevalence, Consequences, and Treatment of Wife Rape,"* www.ncdsv.org/images/nnfr_partnerviolence_a20-yearliteraturereviewandsynthesis.pdf

3. Tario, M. 2016, "Shocking Marital Rape Statistics," www.tariolaw.com/shocking-marital-rape-statistics/

4. Vernick, L. 2007. *The Emotionally Destructive Relationship.* Harvest House Publishers, Eugene, Oregon.

5. *"The Cycle of Domestic Violence,"* http://www.domesticviolenceroundtable.org/domestic-violence-cycle.html

Chapter Nine G-Gratitude

1. **1 Timothy 2:15** (MSG - The Message)
2. Warren, R. 2002. *The Purpose Driven Life: What on Earth am I Here For?* Zondervan, Grand Rapids, Michigan.
3. **Romans 10:9-10** (NLT-New Living Translation)
4. Omartian, S. 1997. *The Power of a Praying Wife.* Harvest House, Eugene, Oregon.

Chapter Twelve U-Unwavering

1. Meyer, C. (2014) *"The Emotional Stages of Divorce: What to Expect During and After the Divorce Process,"* https://www.huffingtonpost.com/cathy-meyer/the-emotional-stages-of-d_b_779816.html
2. Williams, A. 2015. "The Seven Stages of Grief with Divorce," https://www.livestrong.com/article/129455-seven-stages-grief-divorce/
3. Sweet, R. 2000. *A Woman's Guide to Healing the Heartbreak of Divorce.* Hendrickson Publishers, Inc.

Chapter Thirteen S-Stable

1. Stanley, A. *"The New Rules for Love, Sex & Dating,"* http://northpoint.org/messages/the-new-rules-for-love-sex-and-dating

2. Wilson, P.B. 1995. *Knight in Shining Armor: Discovering Your Lifelong Love.* Harvest House Publishing, Eugene, Oregon.

3. Townsend, J. 2011. *Beyond Boundaries: Learning to Trust Again in Relationships.* Zondervan, Grand Rapids, Michigan.

4. *The Shack* (2017). Directors: Hazeldine, Stuart. Producers: Netter, G and Cummings, B.

Acknowledgements

Dreams and visions! These are not possible, nor do they come to fruition, without a whole lot of help and an equally vested group of people. I am so blessed to have you all in my life, and as a part of this literary work. You have no idea how much your support, prayers, and time has been on this journey. One word: PRICELESS!

None of the digging would have been possible to do without the help from my Best Friend, The Holy Spirit. He is truly my Comforter. I am forever grateful for the day I accepted Jesus Christ as my Lord and Savior. My story for Your Glory!

Abbey – Thick and thin, not only my sister but my best friend. "I got your back, SIS!"

Liz – Riding across country, ears are no longer plugged. "Where are we going with this? I need you to take me there!" Personal counseling sessions, early mornings — you name it! Your friendship is a treasure.

Tif – Can't keep baby in the corner. "One more minute: Just say it already!" My sister-friend and book buddy plowing the field.

Lildella - Had you not planted the seed, "You know you need to write your book..." Thank you for encouraging me to do it anyway!

Ericka - Your excitement and creativity are your unique value. Thank you for stepping in and helping with what you do best!

Thank you to the KishKnows Publishing Team. I would not have been able to get this project done had it not been for your excellent level of service.

To Pastor Nancy for encouragement and wisdom through some difficult times.

To my FHC family who have prayed behind the scenes. To my parents it is because of your love for me that I am able to know love. To my brother, I am proud I love you and I am grateful for you. To my Grandmothers, Grandfathers, Aunts, Uncles, sister and cousins: Many moments in my life were a result of our time together. Thank you for those life lessons!

To Pastor Robb and Mrs. Linda, without your faithfulness to preach the uncompromised Word of God, I would not be who or where I am today, I am forever grateful!

To my daughter, the beat of my heart, the reason I do what I do. I love you, to the moon and back!

Resources for Help

If you are like me, Google is your best friend. You are very good at looking for anything and everything on Google. Here I have provided a list of readings and resources to further help you or someone you love. The one thing I want you to know is that you are never alone. My first and best resource is my Bible. I encourage you to read it often! It has given me wisdom, comfort, and guidance.

Recommended Reading List

Eldredge, J. & Eldredge, S. *Captivating Revised and Updated: Unveiling the Mystery of a Woman's Soul.* Zondervan Publishing House, 2010.

Evans, Patricia. *The Verbally Abusive Man: Can He Change?* Adams Media Corporation, 2006.

Evans, Patricia. *The Verbally Abusive Relationship: How to Recognize It and How to Respond.* Adams Media Corporation, 1996.

McDill, S.R. and McDill, L. *Dangerous Marriage: Breaking the Cycle of Domestic Violence.* Spire Press, 1999.

Munroe, M. *Single, Married, Separated and Life after Divorce.* Destiny Image, 2003.

Omartian, S. *The Power of a Praying Wife.* Harvest House, 1997.

Rivers, F. *Redeeming Love.* Multnomah Books, 2007.

Townsend, J. *Beyond Boundaries: Learning to Trust Again in Relationships.* Zondervan, 2011.

Vernick, L. *The Emotionally Destructive Marriage: How to Find Your Voice and Reclaim Your Hope.* Waterbrook Press, 2001.

Vernick, L. *The Emotionally Destructive Relationship.* Harvest House Publishers, 2007.

Warren, R. *The Purpose Driven Life: What on Earth am I Here For?* Zondervan, 2002.

Phone Numbers for Information and Help

Always dial 9-1-1 if you are in danger or in an emergency

National Domestic Violence Hotline
800-799-SAFE (7233)
800-787-3224 (TDD)
www.thehotline.org
English and Spanish, providing crisis intervention and referrals to local services and shelters.

Childhelp National Child Abuse
1-800-4-A-CHILD (224453) 24-Hour
www.childhelp.org/hotline
Crisis intervention and information, literature, and referrals for emergency, social services and support resources.

National Dating Abuse Helpline (For Teens)
866-331-9474 Accessible via text "LOVE IS" to 77054 to talk to peers 24/7. Confidential.
www.loveisrespect.org
Peer advocates, information, and advocacy to those involved in dating abuse relationships, as well as concerned parents, teachers, clergy, law enforcement, and service providers.

National Runaway Switchboard
800-RUNAWAY
800-621-4000
A variety of services are available 24/7

RAINN: Rape, Abuse & Incest National Network
National Sexual Assault Hotline
1-800-656-HOPE (4673)
www.rainn.org

Provides victim services, public education, public policy and training

DoD Safe Helpline
877-995-5247
Provides crisis support service to survivors and family in the Department of Defense community

Family Renewal Shelter
888-550-3915
253-475-9010
This Christian resource provides crisis help and safety planning for victims of abusive relationships.

Lighthouse Network
877-562-2565
www.lighthousenetwork.org
This free hotline provides treatment options for victim and perpetrator for behavioral, emotional, stress, or substance abuse issues, either outpatient counseling, inpatient, detox, or rehab.

Awake, Inc.
www.awakeonline.org
A website that offers various resources and biblical helps for recognizing and stopping destructive relationship patterns.

DivorceCare.org
This organization provides a 13-week course for healing through separation and divorce.

About the Author

Rakisha Vinegar is an educator, writer, and speaker. She holds a Doctor of Education degree and has been studying boundaries in relationships for over ten years. From personal experiences, she has helped many women overcome relational challenges and life setbacks. Her continual pursuit of God and self-awareness have been a guidepost for her life. Dr. Rakisha's motto is "Dare to be R.A.R.E. Refined ~ Ardent ~ Resilient ~ Empowered." She currently resides in Illinois with her teenage daughter.

Join the Movement!

For speaking engagements or for more information, contact Rakisha at:
  www.DrRakisha.com
  Follow Rakisha on Facebook @Dr.Rakisha
  Follow Rakisha on Twitter @rarefined

Unspoken Conversations: A Guided Journal

Full of questions and space for journaling your thoughts and provoke further dialogue, digging to uncover those buried hurts from your past relationships to allow God's love to fully overtake you.
   Available Fall 2018

www.ingramcontent.com/pod-product-compliance
Lightning Source LLC
Chambersburg PA
CBHW071923290426
44110CB00013B/1455